D0021687

CIVIC CENTER

UNBREAKABLE

UNBREAKABLE

My Story, My Way

A MEMOIR

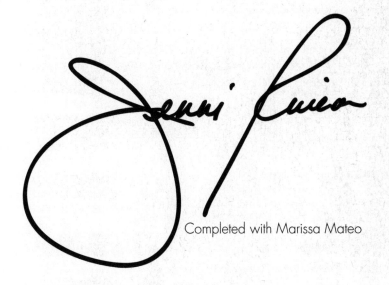

Completed with Marissa Mateo

ATRIA BOOKS

New York   London   Toronto   Sydney   New Delhi

ATRIA BOOKS

A Division of Simon & Schuster, Inc.
1230 Avenue of the Americas
New York, NY 10020

First Atria Books hardcover edition July 2013

ATRIA BOOKS and colophon are trademarks of
Simon & Schuster, Inc.

For information about special discounts for bulk purchases, please
contact Simon & Schuster Special Sales at 1-866-506-1949 or
business@simonandschuster.com.

The Simon & Schuster Speakers Bureau can bring authors to
your live event. For more information or to book an event contact
the Simon & Schuster Speakers Bureau at 1-866-248-3049 or
visit our website at www.simonspeakers.com.

Stage photographs by George Cruz
Personal photographs by Rosa Rivera
Permission to reprint lyrics: "Las Malandrinas," "Dama Divina,"
    and "Mariposa de Barrio" by Cintas Acuario Publishing

Designed by Dana Sloan

Manufactured in the United States of America

10   9   8   7   6   5   4   3   2

Library of Congress Cataloging-in-Publication Data is available.

ISBN 978-1-4767-4607-4
ISBN 978-1-4767-4475-9 (pbk)
ISBN 978-1-4767-4476-6 (ebook)

We want to dedicate this book to YOU.
Thank you for not only taking the time to read
our mother's life story, but for allowing yourself
to feel inspired by the woman we not only love but admire.

A special thank you to all of our mother's fans,
because we know her life wouldn't have been half as blessed
if it wasn't for the love and support you all gave her.
We love you.
Jenni's little soldiers: Chiquis, Jacqie, Mikey, Jenicka and Johnny

Contents

UNBREAKABLE

1

Aren't You El Cinco's Lady?

Ahora estoy, entre luces hermosas
mas cuando estaba sola, sé que Dios me cuidó.

(Now I am among the beautiful lights,
but when I was alone,
it was God who took care of me.)
—from "Mariposa de Barrio"

Sunday, January 26, 1997

The night began at El Farallon, a popular nightclub in Lynwood, California. El Farallon was where you went to hang out with your friends and get lost in the music, forgetting everything else for just a few hours. It was where I met Juan López, my second husband, after locking eyes with him across the dance floor. Most important, it was where many regional Mexican singers launched their careers. And it was where I decided to shoot my first music video, for my song "La Chacalosa" (The Jackal Woman).

My father had done business with the owner of El Farallon, Emilio Franco. Franco said we could shoot the video before the doors opened

1

at 9:00 p.m. At the time, my dad, known to many as Don Pedro Rivera, was one of the biggest producers of regional Mexican music. He had always been my biggest supporter, especially in those early days when I was struggling to break out. He had plans to buy commercial airtime for this video to promote "La Chacalosa."

I wasn't making much money with my music. It was difficult to get my songs on the radio because I refused to fit into the mold of the typical Latina singer. I should have been younger, thinner, softer, quieter, dumber. In the Latino community, female singers were supposed to be beautiful and superskinny, and their music was supposed to be silly. Latina singers were meant to be looked at and not really heard. But I wasn't eye candy. I was considered overweight. I was considered not to have vocal talent. And I was singing strong, ballsy *corridos* (folk tales, often involving drug dealers). I probably intimidated the men. No other women were singing *corridos*. It was like a woman rapping. Women weren't thought to be tough enough, or real enough, to be singing about the gritty world of drug dealers. The people in the industry tried to make me change. If you want to make it in this genre, they said, you have to do this or that. A lot of women had to do sexual favors to get played on the radio. Fuck that. I wouldn't do it. I wanted to make it based on my talent or not at all.

At the time we shot the video for "La Chacalosa," I was working as a Realtor to support my three children and myself. Music was secondary. Juan López, the man I later married, was serving a seven-month prison sentence after being charged with smuggling immigrants. He was set to be released in three weeks. Because I didn't want to be alone, my sister, Rosie, and her friend Gladyz came with me when I would go out at night for a music gig. On this night they sat in the nearly empty club watching me do several takes of the song. I thought we would be done by nine, but by the time we finished taping at around nine thirty, a few customers had started to trickle into the bar area. Before we left I went to the ladies' room. As I exited the restroom, a man grabbed my right arm to make sure he had my attention. "Aren't you El Cinco's lady?" he said. El Cinco (The Five) was Juan López's nickname. I distinctly remember looking into this man's green eyes as he tugged roughly at my arm. He was making me upset and he knew it. "Leave me the fuck alone," I told him as I broke away, wondering how he knew Juan and why he cared if I was Juan's lady.

I picked up my things and walked out of the club with Rosie and Gladyz. I was in a bit of a rush because they were both still in high school, and this was a school night. I wanted to get them home as quickly as possible so we wouldn't get in trouble and they would be allowed to hang out with me whenever they wanted. I was never one to have many friends, especially since Juan scared many of them away with his temper and his rude behavior. Now that he was incarcerated, I was a loner. Hanging out with the girls was fun and helped keep me busy until his release.

First I dropped Gladyz off at her house on Walnut Avenue in North Long Beach, then I dropped Rosie off at our parents' house on Ellis Street, just a few blocks away. It was only 10:30, so we were in the clear. Once I made sure Rosie was in the house, I turned up the music and began the drive back home. I was living in beautiful, gangsteriffic Compton. Being a Realtor, I had bought a house there as an investment and decided to live in it for a while. It wasn't the best neighborhood, but I was happy to have a place to call my own. I couldn't wait to get to my bed that night. I was singing along to my all-time favorite CD, *15 Éxitos*, by Marisela, as I drove down the 91 freeway west.

As I exited right onto Central Avenue, I noticed the car behind me flashing its high beams. It got closer and closer as I slowed down to see if I knew who it was. I didn't recognize the small white sports car and I couldn't see who was driving. The driver flashed his high beams again. What the fuck? Was I driving too slow? Did I forget to turn on my signal? Suddenly, the car sped up alongside my green Ford Explorer, purposely trying to sideswipe me. That's when I realized not just one but three men were in the car, and I started to get scared. I sped up, hoping that they were just messing around with me. They weren't. They would drive behind me, then speed up and try to run me off the road and into the parked cars on Central Avenue. "Shit. What the hell am I going to do?" I said to myself.

I was approaching my house on Keene Avenue and didn't want these men to know where I lived. I was living alone with my three young children. Our house had been broken into just two months earlier, and everything had been stolen. That's how the neighbors had found out that my husband was locked up and wasn't there to protect us. All of this was running through my mind as I kept driving around the block, hoping these guys would magically disappear. My whole body was shaking. Finally, I stopped close to my house, though not in front of it. "Maybe they'll just leave," I kept saying to myself. How foolish.

Their car stopped behind me and I could see that the men were ready to step out. I didn't know what to do, and fear took over. I decided that I would make a run for it. I would run as fast as I could, the way my brothers had taught me to when we played baseball as kids.

I opened my car door and started sprinting in my high heels, screaming at the top of my lungs. I did not look back. I could hear the sound of their boots running after me. I ran, I screamed louder. I cried. I prayed that someone would hear me. If they did, nobody came to my rescue. The boot steps were gaining on me. My high heels were slowing me down. Suddenly I felt two pairs of strong arms grab me. I had been caught. I tried to fight back. I kicked and screamed. I wasn't going out easy. I was the gangsta bitch from Long Beach. The Rivera rebel who never lost a fight.

But I was outnumbered. One man had stayed in the car. One covered my mouth with his huge hand. One dragged me by the hair and pulled at my arms until I was thrown in the backseat of the car. That's when I saw those green eyes again. The prominent chin. The man from the club.

He raped me in the backseat of the vehicle. Over and over he repeated the words I had said to him at the club: "Leave me the fuck alone. Leave me the fuck alone." He mocked me as he raped me. As the tears streamed down my face, I decided not to fight back anymore. All I could think about was my kids. I was so afraid that I was going to be killed and they would be left without a mother. Maybe the men would let me live if I "behaved." I felt that I was losing myself. I could feel the strength seeping out of my body and mind. I was afraid that they were going to take turns on me, but when the man was finished, he told his friend, "Throw this bitch out my car." I silently thanked God as I was slammed onto the sidewalk, realizing that it was finally over. But the damage was done.

I sat on the curb, numb. I couldn't cry. I was just relieved to be alive.

I vowed that I would never tell anyone of my shame. They say that when you keep a secret, it eats you up inside, but I felt that it was better that way. I wanted to appear strong in front of my children and my family. I didn't want anybody to know. And I wanted to maintain my persona as Jenni, the Rivera rebel who had never lost a fight. But deep down inside I knew I had lost a piece of myself that I would never recover. My soul had been shattered, but to the outside world I did just as I had been taught since I was a little girl: I kept my head up and continued forward. It is, after all, the Rivera way.

2

The Rivera Way

Que no hay que llegar primero
Pero hay que saber llegar.

(*You don't have to arrive first*
but to know how to arrive.)
          —from "El Rey"

My father, Pedro Rivera, first came to the United States in the sixties. He left my mother, Rosa, and my two brothers, Pilly (Pedro) and Gus (Gustavo), behind in Sonora, Mexico, with the promise to return for them when he had enough money. He headed to California in hopes that he would find work. He crossed the border illegally with three other men in a dangerous and risky passage. When they finally made it to San Diego, the other men wanted to sleep, but my dad is one of those people who always has to keep working. If there is one thing he doesn't know how to do, it's rest.

Dad left his three companions sleeping in the shade and walked to the nearest gas station. He asked the man at the counter if there was somewhere he could work. The man told him to go to Fresno; that was where the work was at the time. "Great," my dad said. "How do I get there?" The man told him to take the Greyhound bus. The problem was, by the time my father made it to San Diego he had only sixty cents in his pocket, which was not enough to pay the Greyhound fare. When he told the man that he had no money, the man paid for his bus ticket and gave him an extra $20. To this day, my dad cries when he remembers that moment. It changed his life.

So my father followed the man's advice and went to Fresno, where he started to pursue the American dream. He worked in the fields, picking grapes and strawberries. For the first few months, he lived with friends he had met there. He finally saved enough to rent a little apartment and then return to Mexico to get my mother and brothers.

But while my parents were in Mexico getting ready to leave for the United States, my mother became pregnant with me. She was twenty years old and terrified. She was leaving for this new country where she didn't speak the language, they didn't have money, and she already had two young children. The last thing she wanted or needed was another mouth to feed. So she tried, in every way possible, to abort me. She threw herself into burning-hot water. She moved the refrigerator and other heavy furniture, hoping that the pressure and strain would terminate the pregnancy. She drank teas and other home remedies that friends told her about. Nothing worked. Many years later, when I was sitting at her kitchen table and telling her I was about to give up on life, she told me this story. She said that back then she knew that I was a fighter, that I would always be a fighter.

I was born on July 2, 1969, in the UCLA hospital, the first Rivera born on US soil. The hospital was new and they had a program through which it only cost $84 to have a baby. Thank God, since my parents did not have health insurance. When I was growing up, my father would always say I was their cheapest baby. They named me

Dolores, after my maternal grandmother. My middle name was going to be Juana, after my paternal grandmother. Dolores Juana. Can you imagine? Ugliest name ever! My mother had the good sense to say, "We can't do this to her. Isn't there an English version of Juana we can use? Or what about using your cousin's name, Janney?" My father caved and I was christened Dolores Janney. Still not exactly the most beautiful name you've ever heard. I never let my parents off the hook for that one. "I was a baby! How do you give a child a grown woman's name?" I would say. I never went by the name Dolores (though if my brothers and sister wanted to piss me off, that's what they would call me, or Lola). As a child, I was always Janney or Chay.

I was a fair-skinned, redheaded baby. My parents said that when they brought me home my older brothers, who were five and three, instantly fell in love with me. Pilly and Gus were instructed to protect me and care for me. I was "the queen of the house" and "la Reina de Long Beach," as my father said. If anything bad ever happened to me, it was on them. So they treated me as if I were another little boy. Since they had to protect me, they wanted to make sure I was tough enough to defend myself.

Financially, things were not good during those first few years. My parents moved us from Culver City to Carson to Wilmington and then to Long Beach. We were constantly on the move because we were always being evicted. My mother told my father that she would not have another baby until she had her own house. That's when they bought the small two-bedroom on Gale Avenue near Hill Street on Long Beach's West Side. The area was known for gang warfare, but it was the first place where the Riveras finally had a plot of American land to call their own. It was home.

I was almost two when we moved into that house, and my mother immediately became pregnant with her fourth child. Soon after she found out that she was pregnant, she got the news that her father was dying in Mexico. She couldn't go back to see him because there was no money, and because if she crossed over the border again, she might not have been able to come back. One of the dilemmas of pursuing the American dream is that you sacrifice being able to ever see the friends and family you left behind. Back then I never realized how hard it must have been for my mother to be living in this new country, barely getting by financially, with three young children and another on the way. But how could I have known? My mother never let on that anything was wrong. She kept her chin up and acted as if everything were just fine, so we did too.

Mommy would have me rub her belly to get me acquainted with the little girl that was on the way. She wanted to have a baby girl so I could have a sister and we could grow up together and be lifelong friends, just like her and her sisters. It would be perfect. Two boys and two girls. But my mother's wishes didn't come true. She ended up having a little boy with huge brown eyes and beautifully formed lips. They named him Guadalupe Martin Rivera, and he was born on January 30, 1972. As a little boy we called him Pupi, and then later on we called him Lupe.

When Pupi was a baby, I didn't want anything to do with him. When he cried, my mom would say, "Jenni, can you calm the baby?" I would go over to his crib, pat him for a few seconds, and say, *"No ores, no ores,"* which means "Don't pray. Don't pray." I was trying to say *"No llores"* (Don't cry), but I couldn't pronounce my *l*'s. Either way it didn't matter what I was saying, he would never listen to me. He just kept on crying. I'd get frustrated and I would storm out of the room and yell, "Fine! Pray then!" And that's pretty much how our relationship has always been. Because we were so close in age, we shared a special bond. We would get frustrated with one another, we would torture each other (I used to get him naked and lock him outside the house quite often), but in the end we always came together as partners in crime.

My new little brother was an attractive child with a special charm. My mother always reminded us that even though Pupi had my father's body type and character, he looked like her handsome brothers, especially Tío Ramón. I sometimes think that this was why Pupi was her favorite, or at least that's what we all thought. He always received tons of attention from my mom and the rest of us because he was the baby for so long. He was the reigning king for six years until my mother was pregnant once more.

At that point I was nine years old and I was so sick of boys. I told my mother, "You better have a girl." On the day she left for the hospital I said, "If you don't have a girl, don't bother coming back." But out came this beautiful, ten-pound baby boy.

My mother called the house and said to me, "*Mija*, I'm sorry, but the hospital we came to only had boys."

I screamed at her, "Well then, why didn't you go to a different hospital?"

"It was too far away. We didn't have time."

That wasn't a good enough explanation for me. "Don't come back!" I told her, and hung up the phone.

Two days later she returned home with this bundle in her arms, my brother Juan. Lupe didn't want him either. How dare anyone take his title as the baby of the family? Lupe wouldn't even look at him, but I eventually gave in and said, "Fine. Let me see him."

Mom knelt down and pulled the blanket back.

I saw this gorgeous little face. I fell completely in love. "He's beautiful! I'm going to call him Angel Face."

"So we can keep him?" Mom asked.

"Yes, we can keep him."

He was so perfect that I fully forgave him for being a boy, even though this meant I was the only girl in a family of four boys. I became a tomboy by necessity. I never played with dolls because my brothers would ruin them if I even tried. For a while my mother bought me every new doll that she could afford, and within a day or two the boys would cut off its head or arms. They would hide the dolls or bury them in the backyard. My mother would ask me where they went, but I'd never tell. We never told on each other. That was an unwritten rule. Instead, I asked for cars and marbles, just like the boys. One year I even asked for a lawn mower. I learned to play baseball, just like the boys. And I learned to fight, stick up for myself, and take no shit, just like the boys.

By the time I turned eleven, my mother was pregnant once more. On July 2, 1981, the day I turned twelve, I was having my birthday party. It was not exactly a huge affair since the only guests were my parents, my brothers, and two girls from the neighborhood. I was always the oddball and the bookworm, so I didn't have a group of friends to invite. We were just about to cut the cake when my mother's water broke. Everyone sprang into action to get mom out the door while I sat there with my cake and made my wish. "Please, God, bring me a sister," I begged. Hours later, we got the phone call. My wish had come true. I finally got my real-life sister, my baby doll that my brothers could not destroy. At that moment, Rosie was the greatest birthday present that God had ever given me. I adored Rosie like no other and spoiled her in every way that I could. When she was a little girl, she hated to brush her hair and wear clothes, and it would make my mother upset. I would say, "Leave her. Let her be naked. Who cares if her hair is uncombed? It only matters that she is happy." I was her protector and she was my shadow, following me everywhere I went. I made it my mission to shield her from anything bad and give her everything I hadn't had as a child.

⚘

We grew up on the West Side of a racially divided Long Beach, and that meant fighting was a part of life. It was the only way to survive in the barrio. From an early age I remember witnessing the rumbles in the streets. I also remember being aware of the way girls were treated and perceived in the neighborhood.

On my first day of school at Garfield Elementary I saw the boys coming up behind the girls as they bent over to drink from the water fountain. They would grab them by the waist and pretend to hump them. It looked a lot like what the male dogs did to the female dogs in our neighborhood. How gross! That the girls didn't do anything about it made it even worse. I told myself that if any boy ever tried to do that to me, I would knock him out, just as my brothers had ordered.

When I was in first grade, Arturo, the boy I had a crush on, asked me if it was okay to put his hand up my dress. His daddy had told him that was why girls wore dresses and skirts. That was the end of my crush on that little punk and the last time I wore a dress to school. For years my mother would fuss over my tomboy clothes, but I never told her why I refused to wear girlie skirts and dresses. I did tell my older brothers, Pilly and Gus, about Arturo's request. They warned me that they didn't want to hear from their friends that their sister was being "felt up on" by the boys at school. "If we're going to be hearing rumors, it better be that you socked them or kicked them in the balls!" they warned me. "And don't you dare come home crying either!"

I remembered their words one afternoon when I was walking home from school with my mom and Pupi. I was nine and my little brother was seven. My mother was holding Pupi's hand and I was next to them. All of the sudden I felt a hand swipe the bottom of my butt and then work its way up before I turned around to face Cedric, a black boy from the neighborhood. I didn't even think about it. I was swift. All the wrestling my brothers had taught me came in handy. I grabbed him by his Jheri curls and slammed him to the ground, sat on him, and got to punching. I could hear Pupi's cheering and my mother screaming for me to stop. No way! I was enjoying it too much. "Say you're sorry, punk," I demanded. I didn't stop punching until Cedric finally apologized. When I got up, Pupi yelled, "Now stomp on his balls!" So I did.

I soon developed a reputation as "the girl who beats up the boys." But I also fought with girls quite a bit. I was an equal-opportunity brawler. My dad and brothers loved it. Usually whenever a fight started, one of the boys would run into our house and scream to the rest of the family, "Chay is fighting! Come outside." Dad would run outside with my brothers, and all of them would be very scared. Mom would run outside with Rosie, and both of them would be very scared. Mom would be screaming for somebody to stop the fight, but Dad wouldn't let anyone step in. He would say, "Let her learn how to defend herself." I was not a girl who picked fights. I was a nerd, a straight-A student. I usually got along with everyone, but if a boy touched my butt, it was on. I would turn right around and sock him in the mouth and then get him down on the ground and start punching. Nobody was going to touch my ass and get away with it.

And that was precisely what started the big drama of 1983.

One evening in early November, I could hear my mother shouting at my father: "That's it, Pedro. I'm done with Janney. I can't even begin to count how many times I've had to pick her up from school for fighting. It's so embarrassing!"

My mother was furious. I could hear her all the way from the kitchen as she heated up tortillas for my father's dinner. He was sitting in the dining room, listening to Mom's rant while eating. I was in my bedroom right next to them, staring at all the Menudo posters I had pinned to my walls. I loved spending time in there with Rosie and telling her how one day I was going to French-kiss Ricky Meléndez and get my lips stuck on his braces, as if she could really understand what I was talking about at the tender age of two.

Mom wasn't letting up. "Everyone expects a mother to pick up her teenage gangster son for getting in trouble. But who do I walk out of that office with? My daughter. This time she has gone too far. This time she got into a fight with a black boy and it's created a racial problem at school. Everyone is talking about it, and it's causing more trouble than the school officials can handle. They're having a directors' meeting tomorrow and will decide if she will be expelled or transferred to another school. *¡Qué vergüenza!* How embarrassing! I'm not going to show my face this time."

Rosie looked at me. Even she knew Mom was mad at me and something serious was bound to happen. Her beautiful brown eyes were wide open as I told her to shush with one finger over my lips. I didn't want to miss my dad's response.

"You don't seem to fuss much when you go to the awards assemblies and she's getting her outstanding-student awards, do you?" my father said. "You're full of joy when you get notices in the mail letting you know your daughter is the only Hispanic female on the honor roll, aren't you? I don't think you should come down on her so hard when she gets in a little trouble."

"A little trouble!" Mom shouted. "Didn't you just hear me when I said she will most likely be expelled?"

"I know my daughter. I'm sure she had a reason for slapping the crap out of that boy."

That's my daddy, I thought to myself. He always had my back.

So what had happened, exactly? On Halloween Day 1983, a black boy grabbed my ass and I turned around and popped him one right on the mouth. He socked me right back and busted my lower lip. Eddie, a friend of mine who lived on the same street, saw it all. Eddie did what any other boy from our barrio would have done: He punched the black boy in the face and knocked the living daylights out of him. That's the way it was in the hood. We had each other's back. The Mexicans defended the Mexicans. Besides, it was a female who had been hit. It was on now. The racial war at Stephens Junior High had begun. The blacks against the Mexicans. Within weeks it grew into a citywide issue. Blacks and Mexicans were caught in rumbles in all the major junior high and high schools. There were fights throughout the city streets, especially on the West Side. All of this happened for grabbing a girl's ass. Janney Rivera's ass.

I headed to school the following morning wondering what they would do with me. I had a feeling that I wasn't going to be able to finish my ninth-grade year with my best friends, Ruby and Alma, and the rest of our homegirls. The counselors and decision makers at our school were all black. That I was a straight-A student and on the honor roll wasn't going to matter. What mattered was that a Mexican dared mess with one of their own. Sure enough, that morning I was kicked out. And sure enough, my proud father came to get me. We didn't say a word about it on the way home. Instead, my father played the car radio full blast as we listened to Vicente Fernández's "El Rey." We stopped at our favorite place: 31 Flavors. I got a scoop of Jamoca Almond Fudge on a sugar cone as a reward.

I was transferred to Bancroft Junior High in Lakewood Village to complete the rest of my ninth-grade year. Academically, I remained a straight-A student. My behavior, however, changed quite a bit. I found myself surrounded by white girls whose main concerns were their looks and not who was the better fighter. I soon wanted to be, and look, more feminine. My mother was happy to see that her daughter was looking and acting like the young lady she had always wanted. The change also brought on something I wasn't at all used to—attention from boys. My parents weren't familiar with this either. At Stephens, I was the nerd. My friends were all beautiful, and they were the ones getting all the attention from the boys. I was considered the bookworm that everyone respected, but not the girl anyone hit on. At Bancroft, this was no longer the case.

Suddenly I wanted to wear the same Jordache jeans, the Vans, and the Nike Cortez that the other girls were wearing. I mentioned it to my mother and she said we couldn't afford it. For years my mother shopped at the Purple Heart Thrift Store, a secondhand-clothing store on the West Side of Long Beach. But that wasn't what I wanted anymore. With six kids it was not easy to dress us all, and if I wanted to buy expensive clothes, I would have to pay for them myself. However, Mom wouldn't allow me to have a part-time job during the school year. Maintaining good grades was highly important in our house, and nothing was to get in the way of that. I would have to wait until summer vacation to have a job and save up for my new wardrobe.

We didn't have a lot of money growing up. I don't know what kind of person I might have turned out to be if my parents hadn't been so economically challenged. Our financial difficulties and our being such a large family forced my parents to work nonstop to give us a better future.

My father often reminded us that we had to work harder, longer, and smarter than everyone else in this life if we wanted to be successful. He talked almost every day about reaching for the Mexican American dream. Because of this I always knew that there was not just one American dream. In a nation of immigrants, there are countless versions of the dream: the Mexican American dream, the African American dream, the Cuban American dream, etc. I've always thought that was such a beautiful lesson and I've carried it with me throughout my life.

So much of what I learned from my father stayed with me forever. He was a nonconformist. He was a dreamer. He always wanted more. When he started a new job, his goal was to be recognized as an excellent employee by his superiors. He wanted to be known as the best at what he did. He aspired to get to the top of the ladder, and he always accomplished it. He always got what he wanted. For years to come, I would hear his loving but firm voice in the back of my mind as I headed out to my different jobs. That voice is still ingrained in my mind now: "Get up, kids! Find something to do. I don't want to see you guys asleep after the sun comes up. I couldn't care less if it's not a school day. I don't want lazy people living in my house. Wake up, clean the yard, rake the leaves, pick up the dog poop, wash down the walls, ask your mother if she needs help with anything. Do *something*! If you can't find anything to do physically, then get up and *think*. Put your mind to work. The key to success in life is getting up early."

My daddy's words have stuck with me. The men I have been with in my life have either said I'm unstoppable, nocturnal, just plain crazy, or, as one of them put it, "a fucking machine." They never understood why I wouldn't stay in bed with them even when I didn't have school, work, or anything else to do. I never understood why they wanted me to lie there and be a lazy ass like them. It just isn't in my makeup. My daddy made sure of it.

To this day I do the same with my own kids. In the morning I go into each of their rooms clapping like a madwoman: "Time to get up, kiddies! Find something to do! The sun's up, waiting for you!" They hate it. "Mom, what's wrong with you? Go back to sleep!" Chiquis will tell me as she throws her blanket over her head, trying desperately to ignore me. Then Michael will scream from across the hallway, "Be a *real* diva. Wake up at one p.m. And let your kids do the same." I tell them to blame their grandpa.

My father's work ethic became my work ethic. When I was a child, I would accompany him to the Paramount Swap Meet and work at his music stand, or at the taco hut. At every job I had I always made sure to be on time and do my best. At my first real job at the purse-packing factory, I got up at 4:00 a.m. to be at the factory by 6:00 a.m. At my waitressing job at the Golden Star Restaurant, at Kentucky Fried Chicken, and as a video clerk at Video One, I worked with a passion. Just like my father.

I learned as much from my mother as I did from my father; her lessons, however, were very different. My mother, Doña Rosa, or Chamela, as I would call her to get her attention (it still pisses her off and I love it!), wasn't too fond of my accompanying my father to his singing classes when I was ten and eleven years old. She would rather I be studying in my room and playing with other little girls in the neighborhood. But I had no interest in playing with Barbies. I much preferred sitting in on my father's singing lessons with La Maestra Franco in Echo Park—or at the many singing competitions around Los Angeles. This did not sit well with my mother, especially because many of the competitions took place in bars. She thought I was wasting precious time. She wanted me to do something with my brain. She knew her daughter had the smarts to be a doctor, a lawyer, a teacher, anything that would give me a certificate or a degree. That was her idea of making it in life and in the United States. She knew my straight A's and being on the honor roll would take me somewhere.

My parents got into quite a few arguments over this. Of course my daddy wanted me to be recognized as an outstanding student, but he would always remind my mother that I had a talent for singing. "My daughter can one day be like Lucha Villa, Lupita D'Alessio, Rocío Dúrcal, and all the rest of those *cantantes*," he would say. " I am sure that is what her future will be. She has it in her blood, Rosa Amelia. You always talk about how you want her to be an academic scholar, but it's you who sets her in the middle of guests at family parties to sing and dance for everyone. I will be happy with whatever my *reina* turns out to be, but stop trying to fight her talent. Nobody can. *Tiene demasiados huevos como para ser algo normal en esta vida.* God gave her and all the rest of my kids a talent for a reason. Singing is her destiny. One day you will remember my words. You'll see."

My mother would give him a "whatever" look to end the discussion, but when she and I were in the kitchen cooking or washing dishes, she would impart her teachings. "Whatever you do, *mija*, do your best. Be different from everyone. Stand out. *Asegúrate de dejar 'huella' donde quiera que vayas.* You're my first girl. Please try to make me happy and become something. I know your father wants you to be a famous and successful artist, but it's a very difficult career, especially for women. I hear all the stories that go on in that dirty industry. *¡Son puras cochinadas!* You're better off being a psychologist like we've talked about before."

I desperately wanted my mother to be proud of me. I loved bringing her my report cards and outstanding-student awards, but I also wanted to make my father proud. Both of their voices were constantly ringing in my head:

"God gave you a talent for a reason."

"Be different from everyone. Stand out."

"Please try to make me happy and become something."

"Singing is your destiny. One day you will remember my words."

"Whatever you do, *mija*, do your best."

3

Taking the Stage

Por eso desde hoy mismo te digo
Que sigas tu camino.

(*That's why from this very day,*
I tell you, follow your way.)
　　　　　　　　　—from "Besos y Copas"

I was eleven years old. My father and I were sitting at La Tormenta Nightclub in Los Angeles for yet another singing competition. Humberto Luna, the most famous Latin disc jockey at the time, was the master of ceremonies. I was the only child among twelve contestants, including my father, trying to win first place that night. When it was my turn, I walked up to the stage, which was actually the dance floor, and the mariachi was ready to play my song "Besos y Copas." It had been one of Chayito Valdez's greatest hits, and ironically, my mother taught it to me. I had been deciding between that song and Chelo's track "Mejor Me Voy," which was one of my favorites.

But for some reason, I went with "Besos y Copas." My father gave me his full support, telling me, as always, that I could do anything I set

21

my mind to, but on this night I was nervous as hell. I took the microphone, just wanting the whole thing to be over with. But when the music started, I panicked and forgot the words. I wasn't even halfway through the song when I ran out of the room and heard the "you're not good enough" bells ringing. I spent the rest of the night sitting next to our car in the parking lot.

When the contest was over, my daddy came and found me. He was *heated*. I wasn't used to his screaming and scolding me. It was always my brothers who had to deal with that side of my daddy, never me. But, boy, did I get it that night. "I thought you said you were prepared for this, Janney. You always need to be prepared for everything you do in life. Don't just jump into things like a fool. You ran out of there like you were scared of something. Is that what I taught you? *¿No que muy chingona?* Where is the warrior in you right now? *¿Dónde estan tus huevos?*" He went on and on. He didn't stop once we got in the car. The trip home seemed endless. As we drove down the 710 southbound, I thought we would never reach the Willow Street exit.

He wouldn't stop. By the time we made it to the West Side, I had decided that if my singing was going to cause my father to scream at me, I didn't want to do it anymore. I wasn't used to this and I wasn't going to have it. That night my father found out that not only did I have his character and personality, but his balls and attitude as well. I turned and looked at him: "I've never been scared of anything, Dad. Just like I'm not scared of telling you right now that I don't ever want to sing again. I don't want to play this music game that you play. I'm done. I promise you, I will never touch a microphone again. And I will show you that I will become something, even if my voice is not involved. You'll see." By the time I said those last words, I was crying. And even though he didn't show it, I knew he was hurt. I was too. To this day he thinks it is because he yelled at me. It wasn't. I was hurt and sad because I had failed my daddy.

As soon as my father parked the car in the driveway, I jumped out and ran into the house and straight to my room. I didn't even say hello to my mother, who was washing dishes in the kitchen. I cried into my pillow and I contemplated getting Pilly's mini-radio and bumping to George Clinton's "Atomic Dog," just to make my father even angrier. Instead, I listened to him tell my mom what had happened. I thought the conversation was over when my mother said, "I told you, singing isn't her thing."

But it wasn't over. My father got the last words, of course. "*Como chingados no*. She will be back one day. I will never bother her with this singing thing again. I will never insist again. But one day, *ella sola, se dara cuenta que esto es lo suyo*. Her love for music is too great. Without me or anyone pushing her, eventually she will be back. I will just sit here and wait."

As a little girl, no matter where we were living, whether it was the apartment in Culver City, the ever-too-small homes in San Pedro and Wilmington, or the two-on-a-lot house my parents were finally able to purchase in Long Beach, there was always music. My father always had the radio turned to Radio Express, the station that specialized in playing the old-school hits of Vicente Fernández, Ramón Ayala, Pedro Infante, Javier Solís, and all the other greats of that time. My father would sing along to his favorites as he worked on the cars in the yard.

Inside, as my mother cleaned the house, she would put on her LPs and sing along with Chayito Valdez, Chelo, Lola Beltrán, Rocío Dúrcal, and Yolanda del Río. I learned the lyrics, and at the tender age of seven I would sing along to songs about drinking to get over men and spending nights at the bar. On Sundays, I would peek into the living room when my parents were watching Raúl Velasco's weekly show, *Siempre en Domingo*. A few artists stuck with me, and the way Lupita D'Alessio expressed herself vocally and physically always got my attention. I loved how Beatriz Adriana, as she sang her famous ranchera songs, made her eyes dance. I tried to imitate them in the bathroom mirror.

My parents actually met at a singing contest when they were teenagers in Mexico. My siblings and I were constantly surrounded by the music they wanted us to carry within ourselves. We were not allowed to listen to or watch anything but Spanish music and Spanish television at home. However, the neighborhood, the barrio, and my friends introduced me to different types of music. The "homeys" would play what we considered then to be hip-hop music. We'd dance to Zapp and Roger's "More Bounce to the Ounce," "So Ruff, So Tuff," and "I Heard It Through the Grapevine" at backyard barbecues.

I loved to dance more than I loved to sing. Since I was seldom allowed to go out and join my friends at the neighborhood parties or go to the school dances, I would dance at home. Every afternoon I would go into my parents' room and change the Spanish station my father had programmed on his radio to the English stations that played the music I wanted to listen to—the Sugar Hill Gang, Midnight Star, the Tom Tom Club—and that would get me dancing when my parents and brothers weren't looking. Other times, depending on my mood, I would listen to something more mellow. I would find the stations that played Peaches & Herb, Marvin Gaye, and Diana Ross. My father and I were engaged in a permanent battle because I would always forget to change the dial back to his Spanish station.

During the summer of 1983, when I was fourteen, I met a boy named Sergio, my first puppy love. Sergio lived on Summit and Canal, in one of the more dangerous neighborhoods on the West Side of Long Beach. He introduced me to the "oldies but goodies" that all the *cholos* (Mexican thugs) in the neighborhood would listen to and bump on their boom boxes and lowrider cars: Brenton Wood, the Delfonics, Mary Wells, Smokey Robinson. My dad saw me talking to Sergio on the corner of Hill and Sante Fe one day as Sergio walked me to the bus stop on the way to school. I can remember only two times during my childhood when my father hit me. He said he wouldn't lay a hand on "la Reina de Long Beach," but when he did, it was serious. When he came home from work that afternoon, he slapped me across the face so hard I flew across the living room. There was no way his queen would be seen with any *cholos*. They could be my friends, but not my boyfriends. My father warned me that if I didn't stop seeing Sergio, he would force me to drop out of school. To me, nothing was more important than school, so that marked the end of my puppy love with Sergio, but it didn't really matter: he had opened me up to yet another style of music, and that was good enough for me.

At the nearly all-white Bancroft Junior High, I was introduced to yet another musical world. The gringos wouldn't listen to the funk artists that the homeys at Stephens did. Yes, they'd listen to a bit of Michael Jackson, but everyone was a fan of the *Thriller* album back then. When we were on the school bus going back home, they would ask the bus driver to change the stereo dial to the pop stations, and they went crazy over the Police, Depeche Mode, and some singer named Madonna.

During this time I met Alfredo. His brother and my brother Pete played on the same baseball team. Alfredo was my age and he went to DeMille Junior High, down the street from my new school. We stopped taking our respective school buses and would take the city bus to and from school to spend a little time together. He would always carry his Walkman and would share it with me as we sat in the back of the bus. He brought all kinds of tapes with him and introduced me to Duran Duran, disco, alternative rock, and some ridiculous, loud, screaming music that I didn't quite understand. He said it was called "heavy metal."

Alfredo and I had been seeing each other for two months when I found out that he lived on the same street as Sergio. This led to a few fights and to Sergio's stabbing Alfredo in the ribs. I saved them both the trouble of fighting for my honor because around the same time my brother Gus had seen my "rockabilly boyfriend Alfredo" macking with a girl at a quinceañera. I was heartbroken and I broke it off with him immediately. For about a day I thought it was the end of the world. But then, once again, I was happy to have been opened up to even more music through that short-lived relationship. I added Alfredo's cassettes to the rest of the repertoire I had gathered during my childhood and teenage years, and I moved right along in search of my next great love and my next musical awakening.

4

My Early Business Sense

Cuando cumplí los quince años
no me hicieron quinceañera.

(*When I turned fifteen years old,*
They didn't give me a quinceañera.)
—from "La Chacalosa"

The summer of 1984 would change my life forever. I was excited for my birthday, not because I would get a quinceañera, but because it meant that I could finally get a real summer job. It also meant I could have my first real boyfriend, but to be honest, that was secondary in my mind.

Money had always been scarce in our house. But my parents were both hustlers, and they passed that on to all of us children. My parents either worked in factories, owned a bar in the city of Wilmington, or sold music at a record store they owned for a short time on Santa Fe Avenue in Long Beach. After returning home from his nine-to-five job, my dad would head out to the local nightclubs with his Polaroid camera to offer clubgoers a picture for a few dollars. My mother would sell Avon or Tupperware for extra money. They never rested.

As children, my brothers and I witnessed their struggle. It came natural for us to be like them. My brothers would collect aluminum cans from the neighborhood trash bins, and often they would take me along. We'd gather enough to make a little money, which Pete and Gus would split and give Lupe and me a little cut. Sometimes we'd offer the neighbors our lawn-trimming services. We made a little extra cash on the weekends that way. And as far back as I can remember, my parents would go to the swap meets to sell cassettes. They each had a music stand. We used to run back and forth between their stands if a customer asked for a cassette that one of them didn't have but the other did. When I was eleven, I noticed that more people were walking through one particular section of the swap meet, and I decided we needed a third spot in that area. I asked a woman who had a stand there if I could rent a table from her and I would give her a percentage of my sales. "You don't have to give me a percentage," she told me. "Just play good music."

When I was fourteen, I convinced my dad to invest in a button machine so I could make buttons to sell at concerts. The first concert I went to was a Menudo show. The week before, I collected all my pictures of Menudo and made buttons. During the breaks or in the bathroom I would sell them. I sold an entire backpackful and made Dad proud. I would do this at many more concerts later on, and that summer I also got my first true job.

My *tía* Licha, who rented the back house of our duplex, had a job at a factory in Long Beach. The main purpose of the company was to stuff women's handbags with paper to make them look full. Tía Licha spoke to her supervisor about me, and I was hired although I was only fourteen years old. Working in that factory was miserable. The conditions were so bad and the managers were cruel to the workers, who were mostly illegal immigrants who were too afraid to speak up. I would come home smelling of plastic and tell my parents how awful it was. My father was horrified and wanted me to stop working there immediately. But my mother said I could not quit. This would teach me the value of an education, which would keep me from working such an awful job for the rest of my life.

Later that summer, Patty, my brother Gus's girlfriend, spoke to her boss about hiring me. Patty worked as a waitress at the Golden Star Restaurant and was sure I could do the job. I went in for an interview on one of my weekends off from the purse-stuffing job and was hired that very day. I enjoyed being a waitress. The interaction with the customers was so much fun—especially at a hamburger joint such as Golden Star, a place frequented by all types of people. Working there, I always took pride in my customer service and being recognized as a good employee. I waited on tables just as the older, more experienced waitresses did. Few people knew that I was only fifteen years old. I didn't look my age. The tight jeans and fitted T-shirts I was now wearing made me look even older, and my curves were beginning to show more as I started to develop into a young woman. Since Golden Star was located on the Pacific Coast Highway, a busy street that connects Wilmington to Long Beach, it was not unusual to see many truckers come in for breakfast or lunch, and they were not always the loveliest customers to wait on. I learned to deal with them, although some just seemed like horny bastards to me.

One hot afternoon in the final days of that August, work was going as usual. I was being a perfectly polite and hardworking waitress, as I always was. I noticed a man sitting at the corner table, close to the Centipede arcade game. He was glancing at me from afar with a smirk on his face. I approached his table, took his order, and walked away. When I returned with his food, he had a lustful grin on his face.

He looked me up and down. Not only was he smelly and ugly, but he had a problem keeping his hands to himself. All of a sudden I felt his hand touch my rear end. I thought to myself, This motherfucker did not just grab my ass! In a split second I threw his food in his face and told him, "Grab this, *pendejo*." I was fired on the spot for being disrespectful to a customer.

I was upset about losing my job, but proud of what I had done. The summer was almost over anyway. In a couple of weeks I would be a tenth grader at Poly High School. I had saved up enough money to get me some new *garras*. I walked home that afternoon thinking about where I was going to shop for my back-to-school clothes and realizing how, once again, my ass had gotten me in trouble.

I continued doing well in school that year. I wanted to make my mother as happy as my brothers did. When I got home from school, I would wash dishes, clean the house, and iron baskets of clothes. She swore I would purposely break the dishes and make a lot of racket with the pans so she wouldn't ask me to do them anymore, but in truth I was only trying to wash them as fast as she did. She had such a great technique and I kept trying to get it down. Although my mother never knew it, I wanted to be just like her. Yes, I was a tomboy. But I also wanted to cook like her, clean like her, work like her, and someday be an excellent mother and wife . . . just like her.

My parents would seldom let us hear their fights. My brothers and I never witnessed any physical violence at home. I never heard of any cheating or any big arguments. At times, however, I would notice that my mother's eyes were puffy and swollen after walking out of their bedroom. I wondered what was wrong, but never dared to ask. Was she upset because money was scarce? Would my daddy dare hit her? Did she find out that he had cheated? I didn't know. What I admired most about my mother was that no matter what, through thick and thin, she had my daddy's back. She was a soldier for their love.

She didn't know it, but she was a proper gangster wife, as we used to call it in the hood. My father was her first boyfriend, her first love, the first man she gave herself to, and the man she stayed with, no matter what. She was not going to raise her children without a father. I loved my mommy's strength and determination to make the relationship work. I vowed that when I grew up, I would be just like her. She set an example that I wanted to follow, an example that would affect my life more than I could even imagine.

5

My First Love

I never wanted to be your weekend lover.
I only wanted to be some kind of friend.
—from "Purple Rain"

In the fall of 1982 I was in eighth grade at Stephens and first met the man who would later change my life. I was walking home from school with my girlfriends Ruby and Alma. They wanted to stop by the Pioneer Chicken Stand on the corner of Santa Fe Avenue and Willow Street to see if they could get a free combo meal from a friend who worked there, Trino, short for Trinidad. When we got there, he looked at me in a way that made me a bit nervous. He asked me my name as I shyly lowered my face to the ground. I looked up at his beautiful, hazel eyes lined by long, dark eyelashes. "Janney," I responded, feeling myself turn pink in the cheeks.

"I like your friend," he told the girls.

At the time he was nineteen and lived in the apartment next door to Ruby's house on Parade Street. Ruby was my best friend and I would be allowed to visit her on the weekends or after school as long as Pupi came along with me. I would see Trino around sometimes

33

during the next few years. According to Ruby and Alma, he was the hottest thing on the block. He would always make an effort to talk to me and get my attention. Once, he told me that every time he heard "Así te quiero yo . . . inocente y sencilla" by Los Yonics, he'd remember me. "I love your innocence," he'd say. "You're such a simple girl. One day you will be my wife." He said that at thirteen I was still a little too young for him. "When you're a bit older, we'll talk about it again."

When I was thirteen and fourteen, I had my puppy loves with Sergio and Alfredo while Trino became Gus's friend and would come over to our house sometimes. My dad warned Gus and my other brothers about bringing guys over to the house: "You open the doors of your house to your friends and they take your sister or your wife." He still believes that to this day. Because of this, Trino stopped coming over, but one way or another, call it destiny, the devil, or God's will, our paths crossed again one day on Parade Street. On that day in 1984, it wasn't Pupi walking with me to my friend's house, but a beautiful, blond living doll—my little sister, Rosie, who was almost three years old. I remember how cool and charming he was and how I was so infatuated with him. Now my stomach turns at the thought of finding Trino so attractive. My story with this man is horrific, but of course it did not start out that way.

By June of that year, Trino and I had started to see each other in secret. I thought he was incredibly attractive. He dressed like a rebel and listened to Spanish rock. He was very charismatic, funny, a good storyteller. Most people who met Trino liked him instantly. I know I did.

On July 2, I turned fifteen. I wasn't able to have the traditional quinceañera that most Mexican families have for their daughters. We couldn't afford it. My daddy made a deal with me. I had a choice between my parents' somehow getting the money to pay for a quinceañera, or my getting a car later when they could afford it. Of course I went for the car (which I never got). Meanwhile, my celebration was to dress up in my fanciest dress and take a ride, top down, in my dad's old convertible.

I felt like a princess sitting on top of that beat-up car, cruising with my daddy, my hero, through the streets of Long Beach. I now realize this was my daddy's way of confirming to me that I was, as he always called me, not the princess, but "la Reina de Long Beach." I was so content and happy.

However, my daddy wasn't too happy when the ride was over. I told him that since I was now "of age," Trino wanted to come over and talk to him about officially dating me. Back in those days, the custom was for boys to meet with a girl's parents and ask for permission, face-to-face, to date their daughter. I thought it was so manly of Trino. Although I had been "seeing" Alfredo previously, my parents okayed Trino's request, and I considered this to be my first true relationship. Actually, he became my first true everything. I was perfectly convinced that he was "the love of my life." *¡Pobre mensa!*

One day, during "visitation time," my father caught Trino and me kissing under the avocado tree. I guess that must have been hard for him to see. When I came in the house, my father stopped me at the dining-room table before I went into my bedroom. "*¡Janney, si te va a chingar!* This motherfucker is going to screw you!" he told me. Daddy knew that, at age twenty-one, Trino's intentions were not on the same level as my teenage desires.

That September I started high school at Long Beach Polytechnic High. Even though it wasn't in the best neighborhood, everyone I knew wanted to go to Poly High, "the home of scholars and champions." My brother Pete had graduated from there in June, Gus had attended temporarily (before getting kicked out for punching a teacher). So had baseball player Tony Gwynn and tennis legend Billie Jean King, among many other famous alumni. When Lupillo was there, a few years later, Snoop Dogg and Cameron Diaz were also students. Of course we didn't know any of them would become such huge stars then. One day, I thought, they will say that Jenni Rivera went here too.

I was doubly excited to go to Poly because it meant I would be reunited with all of the friends I'd left behind at Stephens Junior High when I got kicked out. Finally, I would be able to hang with all the homeys, the Mexicans, Samoans, Filipinos, Guamanians, blacks—all of those people who were just like me: a minority. We would kick it together at lunch, or in the middle of periods, and after school, since during the day I didn't have any classes with my friends. I was in the "nerd classes," as they put it. The only class I shared with a few of them was band. I played clarinet and reached first-clarinet status for the Long Beach Unified School District. I was getting straight A's in all of my "nerd classes" and looking forward to everything that high school had to offer.

But in November everything came to a stop.

The story begins on a warm September night. Trino and I, and our chaperone, my younger brother Pupi, went to a drive-in movie to watch Prince's *Purple Rain*. Halfway through the movie, Trino sent Pupi to the snack bar to get popcorn and candy. It happened right there in the back of his 1979 Monte Carlo. I can't say he forced me because, obviously, I enjoyed feeling his touch, but I got scared and asked him to pull out before he had completely penetrated me. I figured since I didn't feel anything, nothing had happened. In reality, everything had happened. November came around and I still hadn't gotten my period. I wondered if I could have gotten pregnant by the Holy Spirit. Was that still possible? I was so naive and stupid. Or maybe I was just in denial. Yes, I had learned about sex and pregnancy in health class, but I did not want to face the truth. It couldn't be. Wasn't it supposed to feel good and be an unforgettable experience like what I'd heard all the girls talk about at school? Not in my case. Not a chance in my crazy life. I had become pregnant from the precum.

I was in a folkloric dancing class with Patty, my brother Gus's girl-friend and now wife. One afternoon I didn't show up and Patty asked Gus where I had been. I had gone to a clinic to get a pregnancy test. When I came home that afternoon, Gus wanted to know where I had been during dance class. I had no choice. I had to tell him. He broke down in tears when he heard the news. "How can it be? How can you do this to our family? This wasn't the way it was supposed to be, Jan-ney." He told me I had to tell Pete. I couldn't do it. I couldn't face him. I left the house before he came home from work that night.

Soon after, I sat with my mother and gave her the horrible news. It was a great disappointment to her and an extremely sad moment for a fifteen-year-old girl such as me. I didn't know then that Lupe, who was twelve at the time, had been sitting in my bedroom, listen-ing to the whole conversation. As was customary in Mexican culture in those days, I wasn't going to be able to live at home anymore. I would have to move in with Trino and we would have to get married. My mother was scared of what my father might do, so she had me leave before he got home. I had to pick up my clothes and whatever belongings I was going to take with me to my new home while my little brother and sister Juan and Rosie were watching. They were too young and innocent to know what was going on, but Lupe knew ex-actly what was about to happen. After I gathered my things in a black plastic trash bag, I gave my angry mother a kiss and hug good-bye, and I headed out the door and toward the driveway where the father of the child I was carrying awaited.

I took one step out of the front door of my childhood home, and then Lupe stormed out of my bedroom crying, screaming, pleading with my mother not to let me go. "No, Mom!" he sobbed. "Please don't make her go. I don't want to be here without my sister. She can stay in

her room and the baby can stay with us in the garage. It will be okay."
He was inconsolable. My mother looked at him and began to cry as she
brought her hands to her face. She couldn't say a word. Lupe wouldn't
give up. He grabbed me tightly by the arm, looked me in the eye, and
begged, "Please stay with me, Janney! Please don't go!" I'll never forget
the look on his face, the fear in his voice, his words, and the rivers of
tears that rolled down his cheeks. As I type these words, I am crying
remembering how badly he tried to hold me back on the night that
changed my life forever. Did he, at the age of twelve, sense the kind of
situation in which I would soon be living? Did he have a premonition
about how my life would be with this man? I didn't know, but sometimes I think my brother sensed that this man would be at the root of
the Rivera family's most tragic and painful experience.

I dropped my bag on the ground to hug him. I continued crying as
I kissed him good-bye. I picked up my belongings and walked over to
Trino. I left Lupe crying at the front door of our house in Long Beach.
I left my baby sister and brother with no clue as to what was going
on. I left Pete and Gus so disappointed and heartbroken. And I left my
mother, who was so angry and hurt that she could barely speak. I got
into the beige Monte Carlo that would drive me to his family's home
in Wilmington, the city I once lived in as a little girl, and I began a life
nobody would have hoped for "the Reina de Long Beach." Years later
I found out that when my father came home from work that day and
asked where I was, my mom told him I had run away with Trino. Dad
was so upset, and for the next three days he continually asked Mom
if I had called. On the third day she told him the truth. He went into
his bedroom to turn on the radio, and for the first time in a long time
it was tuned to his Spanish station. I hadn't been there to change it.
He cried that night as the music played, for he knew that I was gone
forever. Life would never be the same for our entire family. It certainly
wouldn't be the same for me.

Trino and I were living in the garage in the back of his family's house on Blinn Avenue in Wilmington. He was the only man in a house full of women. The thing was, his mother and all his sisters hated me. They all thought I wasn't good enough for him because I was an American girl. In their eyes all American girls were whores, and Trino should have married a Mexican girl from their ranch. They treated me badly, but that was nothing compared to the shit Trino put me through.

Our garage apartment became the boxing ring for the many verbal and physical fights we would have during our eight-year relationship. Those walls would witness the first tears I shed as a married woman and the tears that would continue to flow for years to come. He had only brought me to live with him because he wanted to show everyone he was a responsible man and he didn't want to publicly disgrace me and my family. But Trino insisted that the baby was not his. He didn't believe the story the doctors gave us. In his mind, I couldn't possibly be pregnant without our fully "doing it." Not only that, he said no woman of his was going to continue to attend school. Trino wanted me to drop out and stay home and be a full-blown housewife. "What about my grades and my education?" I asked. "What about my future and how important it is to accomplish something and be my family's pride and joy?"

"That's done and over with," he responded. "I'm already doing enough by having you here after you slept with someone else and got yourself pregnant. I won't put up with my woman going to school as if she were still a normal teenager. That's not the way it happens in my family, and that's not the way it's going to be with me."

I couldn't believe it. What the hell had I gotten myself into? As the days went on, I kept insisting, thinking I could convince him to change his mind. I couldn't. Instead, I learned what it felt to be slapped in the face by a man. "Oh no, you didn't, motherfucker!" I yelled at him as soon as he did it. I was fucking pissed. I immediately fell back into my tomboy ways and did what I had been trained to do: I fought back.

"I ain't scared of you, you little bitch," I said. "I'll fuck you up!" Obviously, I couldn't do so. He was stronger than me. That was not the last time he slapped me in the face. It happened more times than I would like to admit. But I'd enjoy getting back at him when I'd catch him off guard. I would wait until he was asleep and beat his ass. This was the way our relationship went for years to come. The women in my family used to tell me, "You aren't supposed to do that. You are supposed to let them hit you." My nana was this old-school, religious little lady, and our grandfather used to hit her while she just looked down at the ground and took it. I told her, "Fuck that, Nana. If he hits me, I'm going to hit him back."

Eventually I got my way after much arguing and not giving in to his macho, idiotic ways, and I took my pregnant ass to Reid High School, the continuation high school down the street. Reid specialized in educating the more troublesome students and the pregnant teenagers. In addition to my regular academic classes, the teachers there would prepare me for childbirth.

I'm glad I persisted, because at that school I learned about what was going on in my pregnant body. Ms. McFerrin, my home-economics and child-development teacher, would always remind me that I had to be a happy pregnant girl. She said, and actually showed me in the different textbooks, that a human being's personality is formed in the womb. She assured me that what I put the fetus through during pregnancy would mold my child's character for life. I believed her and later had full proof that it was true.

Three months after I left my parents' house, they were begging me to move back. Despite life with Trino being a living hell, I wouldn't do it. They had kicked me out and I was too proud and stubborn to turn around and forget what had happened. No, I was going to stick it out,

I was going to make things work. I was going to be a gangster wife, just like my mommy.

Our first daughter, Janney (later to be nicknamed Chiquis), was born on June 26, 1985, six days before my sixteenth birthday. Despite Trino's accusations, she looked just like him. I brought her home to my parents' house on July 1 during Rosie's fourth birthday party. They were about to cut the cake when I walked in holding this beautiful green-eyed baby. Rosie was pissed. She had always been my baby and was not too happy that she was being replaced. I promised her that I would never leave her. I assured her that she was still my baby too.

Everyone fell in love with Chiquis, especially her Tía Rosie.

Trino and I moved into the back house on my parents' lot so my mother could help me with Chiquis while I worked my shift at Kentucky Fried Chicken or went to school. Unfortunately this also meant that my family witnessed a lot of the ugly altercations between Trino and me even though I tried to keep them secret.

I gained eighty pounds during the pregnancy, and Trino told me I was now too fat to be his woman. He was constantly calling me names and humiliating me about my looks. I felt so ugly, fat, and worthless, but I never wanted to let anyone else know this. In my family they always called me "unbreakable," and I never wanted to shatter this image of myself. On the outside I kept my head up and maintained my tough-girl image. However, inside I was dying. Because I wanted nothing more than to shut Trino up, I began fad dieting and had lost all the excess weight about a year and a half after Chiquis was born. But then he became jealous and obsessive. I just couldn't win.

By the last few days of January 1987, Trino and I were living in a trailer home we had purchased in Carson. I was working as a cashier at Video One on Willow Street. This was during the time of the VHS craze, and the place was always full of customers, many of them men. One day I received a bouquet of flowers at work. I stupidly thought it was a message from Trino trying to make up after yet another fight. When he came to pick me up that night, I jumped in the car and gave him a kiss, thanking him. In the blink of an eye he slapped me across the face and the flowers flew out the window. That night, I didn't even try to fight back. Instead, I cried myself to sleep and felt myself falling deeper into a depression. I never did find out who sent me those flowers.

The following day I skipped school, but went to work as usual. We needed the $3.75 an hour and I didn't want to be irresponsible. Trino harassed me that evening by calling the video store nonstop. As the phone calls increased, my boss, Kim, a Korean businessman who was demanding and unkind, started to get upset. I was working with my friend Veronica, and each time the phone rang, we grew more anxious. I didn't want to take any more shit from Kim or from Trino's dumb ass. Remembering the slap across the face from the night before and the new accusation that I was sleeping around, I decided to go forward with what had been on my mind. I had been having suicidal thoughts.

I said to myself, "This is it. I can't take it anymore. I need to get away from this man. I love him, but he hurts me too much." I desperately wanted to end the relationship, but I also wanted to be like my mother. I wanted to stay with him and make it work for my daughter's sake, for my own stupid pride, and the old-fashioned belief that I should belong to the same man for the rest of my life. Just like my mommy.

I debated the issue for a long time; I thought about my daughter, my parents, my brothers and sister, and then I thought about myself. I don't remember ever having been so selfish before. During my break, I went to the Alpha Beta Supermarket, which was a couple of doors down from Video One. I bought as many over-the-counter drugs as I could afford and returned to the video store. I walked in, kissed

Veronica on the cheek, and headed straight to the bathroom. There, in the Video One restroom, I downed every single pill in those seven containers, a mixture of everything they had in stock that day. Before I lost consciousness I felt the tears roll down my cheeks. I whispered to the tile floor, "I'm sorry, Mommy, I'm sorry, Daddy."

When I opened my eyes, I was in a bright, white room. It smelled sterile and clean, and I could hear people running back and forth in the hallway. Then I turned to see my parents, and I will never forget the sadness and grief on both of their faces. My mommy cried while my daddy tried, as usual, to show his strength. A heavy teardrop fell down his face as he forced a smile. "You're okay, *mija.*" I didn't know if he was trying to comfort me or if he was trying to convince himself. "Everything is going to be okay," he whispered. "We're going to take care of you. We're going to get you right."

"Don't ever do this to me again, *mija,*" my mother sobbed. I began to cry too when I realized what I had done.

They didn't ask me why. They didn't interrogate me. They didn't want to make me feel worse than I already did. I didn't say anything either. I promised my mother, silently, that I would never do it again.

The next day I was discharged from Pacific Hospital in Long Beach with the order to be admitted into the Los Amigos Rehabilitation Center in Downey. My father's medical insurance wouldn't pay for my expenses at the hospital or at the rehab center. Although my parents never told me, I think they knew that I was losing my childhood warrior spirit. Indeed, I was. I spent two weeks at Los Amigos while my daughter stayed with my parents. As the youngest patient there and the only one to have attempted suicide, I received quite a bit of attention from the other patients, most of whom were suffering from drug and alcohol abuse. The staff had heard about my success in school and that I was a teen mother. They made it a point to rebuild my self-esteem and to make sure I knew how much I had going for me. Trino never showed his face while I was there.

At Los Amigos I first heard the serenity prayer: "Dear God, please grant me the serenity to accept the things I cannot change, the courage to change the things I can, and the wisdom to know the difference."

On the day I was discharged, I silently repeated that prayer to myself on the way back to my parents' house. My brother Pete was driving, my mother sat in the passenger seat, and I sat in the back. Pete kept looking at me through his rearview mirror as "Lean on Me" played on the radio. I felt ready to face the world. I was ready for a fresh start, and I had a new outlook on life. I was finally determined to leave Trino for good.

After Los Amigos, my daughter and I stayed with my parents. I took it day by day. I made it through February without getting back with Trino. Then March. I made it through the entire spring. I was focused on going to school and being a good mother to Chiquis, who was now almost two years old. That June I graduated from high school, and I was the valedictorian of my class. I was offered eight different college scholarships. Trino came to the ceremony and afterward pleaded with me, once again, to come back home to our trailer in Carson.

"Not tonight," I told him. "I'm going to grad night."

"You're not taking me?" he asked.

"I guess not, since I have a date," I responded proudly. "Three's a crowd, baby. We'll talk another day."

I jumped on the school bus with my date, Al, and the rest of the seniors. It was my first time at Disneyland. For one night I felt like a normal teenager.

6

Why Are You Crying, Baby?

If the teardrops ever start
I'll be there before the next teardrop falls . . .
                    —from "Before the Next Teardrop Falls"

I wanted to take advantage of the scholarships I had been
offered, and so that summer of 1987 I began taking classes at Long
Beach City College. Though I was focused on my studies and goals,
guess what? Yup. I did it again. I took him back. I went back to the
"I want to be like my mom" spirit. Back to the violence and the fist-
fights. Back to the loud arguments, another year of the never-ending
screaming and boxing matches. I became concerned about Chiquis
living in this unstable environment and how it was affecting her. I
decided to leave the trailer in Carson that I had helped pay for. To me
the lost money was worth my freedom. So, at the end of 1988, I packed
up and took my daughter back to my parents' house in Long Beach.
As a mother I learned to put aside my pride and do what was best for
my child, even though this meant admitting failure in my marriage. I
was only nineteen years old.

For about two months my life was stable and quiet without Trino in it. But then my world came crashing down again. It was February 11, 1989. I was leaving my job at the Wherehouse Music Store at the Long Beach Mall. I could sense something bad was going to happen. I had stayed overtime to do stock count and had left a bit late that night. At about 10:15 p.m. I was walking through the empty parking lot toward my 1986 Toyota Supra. I heard a pair of quick footsteps coming toward me from behind. It was Trino. "I want us to talk," he said. I argued with him before I finally agreed to discuss things with him. We sat in his Nissan Maxima talking for a while before he began kissing me. *¡Ahí va la pendeja!* I wanted him to stop when things got heated, but he wouldn't. "You asked for it! You can't mess with me like that!" he yelled at me. Fearing that I would make things worse, and because I hadn't gotten any in a while, I gave in. I can't blame it all on him. I was stupid enough to put myself in that predicament. I asked him to use protection or pull out. Since I wasn't sexually active, I wasn't using contraception, but I had learned about the ovulation method and I was positive I could get pregnant that day. So Trino ignored my pleas and with an evil look on his face said, "Fuck that!"

That night I went home knowing that we had conceived another child.

So I was once again living at my parents' home and pregnant. I contemplated having an abortion, but one day, as I sat in my bedroom attempting to do my homework, my mother walked in my room and found me crying. I told her the truth. Considering what I was thinking, I am glad I did.

"You can't have an abortion," she said. "I won't let you do it. It wouldn't be fair to a life that God has planned for. Believe me, one day you will appreciate my advice."

That day I decided to keep the baby, but not wanting to face my father with the news, I also decided to move back in with Trino. I packed up my belongings and headed to the trailer park in Carson with my four-year-old daughter. When I knocked on the door of the trailer, Trino answered and immediately asked me what I was doing there. I told him I was pregnant and couldn't take advantage of my parents any longer. I knew they were disappointed in me and I wanted to show them that we could work things out.

"You can stay," Trino said, "but don't hold me responsible for what-ever might happen."

He didn't want us there. He seemed to be having too much fun being a bachelor and had no interest in married life anymore. How-ever, he did have an interest in belittling me, calling me names, and trying to stop me from achieving my goals. He told me I would never complete my associate's degree that year because I was pregnant and depressed. I put up with more from him during that time than ever before in our relationship. I was committed to making it work, but I was also committed to proving him wrong. I wasn't about to let him win.

We fought constantly. It would start with a screaming match and would quickly escalate. I made sure to run to Chiquis's bedroom be-fore the fights became physical because I feared for my unborn child. Oftentimes Rosie, who was eight years old by then, would spend the night with us. She had grown close to Chiquis. They would both have terrified looks on their faces when I would run into the room and slam the door behind me when Trino was about to hit me.

The fights continued until one day in July of 1989. Trino and I were arguing when he began to beat me. I tried to run away, but I was five months pregnant and couldn't move quickly. He kicked me in the stomach, trying to hurt the baby. I didn't want to scare Chiquis, so I tried not to yell, but when he kicked me again, much harder this time, I couldn't hold it in. I screamed in pain and Chiquis ran out of her room to see if I was okay.

I saw my daughter's face, and that was the breaking point. I could no longer allow my Chiquis to be emotionally scarred and my unborn child to be physically endangered.

Not knowing where I was going, I left that night holding a blanket in one hand and my daughter's hand in the other. I thought we would be sleeping in my car somewhere, since I was not about to go back to my parents' house. I didn't want them to see me in that condition. I drove to my brother Gus's house on Arlington Street on the West Side of Long Beach. Patty and Gus took us in and let us sleep in their living room. Since it was only a one-bedroom house, I knew we could not stay there long. The next day I asked if I could rent out their garage. Although the floor was cement and the ceiling wasn't finished, it had a full bathroom, and that's all we needed. I bought a mini-refrigerator and a small microwave, and financed a bedroom set. A few days later I went back to that trailer park on 228th Street only to pick up our belongings.

I had received my associate's degree in June of 1989 and decided to take that summer off from school. In September I went back to Long Beach City College to complete a few classes before I enrolled at Cal State Long Beach the following semester. I had also started a new job at the Willow/Daisy branch of the Bank of America. Chiquis was enrolled at Young Horizons Child Care Center in downtown Long Beach. Despite the sadness I carried around with me, I felt that I was doing okay. I was moving forward. I didn't want to let our situation get to me. I couldn't let my daughter see me cry any longer. I constantly assured her that we were okay and that things would get better. In a way, I was trying to convince myself, because at that point, whenever I took a step forward, it seemed as though life was pushing me five steps back.

One night when we were living in my brother's garage, I woke up to the sound of someone starting my car. I got up to look out the window. Soon Chiquis woke up and was standing by my side. We watched helplessly as two masked men stole my little Honda. I was seven months pregnant and standing beside my four-year-old daughter in that cold garage apartment. I couldn't move. I stared into the darkness as I recalled that I had nothing but liability insurance on that car. The theft would not be covered. I couldn't afford a new car. I was barely getting by as it was. What the hell was I going to do now? I had to get to work and school. I had to get Chiquis to day care.

I must have been lost in my thoughts for a while; then I felt my daughter softly tugging at my pajamas. "Mommy. Mommy, listen to me." I looked down at her beautiful face. "You let them borrow it, right, Mommy? They're going to bring it back in the morning so you can take me to school, right?" I fought back the tears as I looked into her eyes, those green eyes I so dearly loved. At that moment I wanted to see the world through those eyes so badly. I wanted to be young and innocent and believe in the good of the world. But I had to be strong for my babies. That night, after filing a police report, I lay in bed thinking about how I would pull through for my daughters. I was having another girl, so the ultrasound had shown. I would not let the three of us down. The three musketeers, I thought, trying to smile. But instead I quietly cried myself to sleep, making sure my baby couldn't hear my sobs.

I could have gone to my parents and brothers for help. They would have given me everything they had if I had asked them, but my pride would not allow it. Deep inside I felt that I had to prove—to myself and the world—that I was strong enough to make it on my own. I wanted so badly to be an example of strength for my little girl. At that moment I was down, but one day I was going to be on top of the world with my daughters by my side. With or without my man, I was going to make them proud to have me as a mother. And I was going to make my parents proud, once again, to have me as a daughter.

The following day I called in sick to work and skipped class. I took Chiquis with me to purchase a ten-speed bike. I found a used child seat for her and strapped it to the back of my new vehicle. That bike would be my means of transportation until I could save enough money for the down payment on another car. But this bike wouldn't be as easy to steal. I didn't dare leave it outside. I parked it where it belonged, right next to my daughter and me in the garage. Home sweet home.

The desperation and desire I felt during this time was almost overwhelming. I knew I had to call upon the lessons from my past to get through it all. I reminded myself that I couldn't change my situation immediately, so I learned to live with it and live through it, just as the counselors had taught me in the rehab center. I reminded myself that I had to be a fighter and never stay down, just as my brothers had taught me. I called upon the faith I'd learned from my mother and the Victory Outreach Youth Group I'd joined during my senior year of high school when I felt so lost and alone. And I appreciated all of my father's early-morning wake-up calls, because they gave me the tools I needed for what I had to do.

I got up at four o'clock every morning. I got dressed. I woke Chiquis and got her ready. Then I would strap her into the child seat and I'd ride my bike to downtown Long Beach to drop her off at the day-care center. Next I would ride across town to Long Beach City College to take my classes. After class I rode to Willow Street to make it to my job at Bank of America. I rode that bike as though I were training for a race while my daughter cheered me on from the back. I'd turn to look at her during every single one of those trips. Sometimes I would notice her eyes had turned watery during the cold mornings.

"Why are you crying, baby?" I'd ask.

"I'm not, Mommy, it's the wind hitting my eyes," she'd say.

I still wonder if she was telling the truth. I just knew that she was like her mommy, a gangsta baby.

Toward the beginning of November my father somehow found out about my situation (I am sure from one of my siblings) and asked me to come home until the baby was born. I agreed, and Chiquis and I moved back in for those last few weeks of my pregnancy. I was once again living in my childhood bedroom, and my father would sit by the side of my bed. He couldn't bear to see me cry alone, so he would cry with me. I would feel secure with my daddy, my hero, by my side. Chiquis was just happy to live in the same house with Tía Rosie.

A year earlier my father had established his own record label, Cintas Acuario Music. He produced popular regional Mexican artists, including the now iconic Chalino Sánchez. My parents were doing much better financially, and I was so happy that my baby sister was living a childhood of plenty. My mother used to apologize to me because I didn't have the same luxuries, but I would tell her, "No, Mami, get her the best of everything. Spoil her." I never thought, Why did Rosie get this and I did not? Instead I told myself that one day I would be able to provide this much for my daughters too. Maybe more.

My second daughter, Jacquelin, was born on November 20, 1989. She was this skinny, fragile baby as a result of the circumstances we had lived through while I was pregnant with her. I rode my bike for miles every day. I hardly ate or slept. I was depressed and cried all the time. Yet, from the moment she was born, Jacqie had this beautiful, joyful spirit. My mother said that I should have named her Dulce (Candy) because she was so sweet.

Now that I had two babies depending on me, I knew I had to start making better money. I was determined to get out of my parents' house and into a place of my own as soon as possible. While working at the bank, I noticed that some customers continuously made large deposits to their accounts.

One day I asked one of these customers what he did for a living. He said he was a real estate agent for one of the realty offices in the area.

Immediately, an idea sparked in my mind. I wanted to make the kind of money he was making. I decided to quit school temporarily and enroll at Anthony's Real Estate School in Torrance. Four months later I had my license and was hired at the Century 21 offices on Pacific Avenue. Few Hispanic women worked in real estate, so I recognized that I could fill that void. I would pay Chiquis and Rosie to pass out flyers in the neighborhood to potential real estate clients, and in my first month I sold six homes, which was unheard of in that office. With that money I was able to purchase my first home on Fifty-Fifth Street in Long Beach. I was twenty years old.

Stupidly, during the time I was in real estate school, I began to see Trino again. For a smart person, I can be a real dumbass sometimes. But I was in love with him. He was the father of my children. He was the only man I had ever been with, and so, despite all of his faults, I still thought I could make it work.

He moved into the house on Fifty-Fifth Street, and for a while we did make it work. Things were good between us for a year or so. Through my contacts at work he was able to get a job as an entry-level loan officer. I introduced him to the business and he got busy at work, so we didn't have much time to fight. I thought we were finally on stable ground, so when I found out I was pregnant with our third child, I was happy. I wanted to have a boy, and on September 11, 1991, I got my wish.

While I was in labor with our son, Trino went to the car and fell asleep. Almost instantly, I went from being five centimeters dilated to ten. The nurse came in to check on me and said, "You are ready. Don't push yet. I'll get the doctor." But my baby boy did not want to wait. As soon as the nurse left the room, I delivered my son all by myself. I was there with my baby, his umbilical cord still attached, and I felt so alone.

"It's just me and you, little boy," I told him. Soon I realized the truth of those words. My son was not going to have his father in his life. We named him Trinidad, after his father, but years later he would change his name to Michael, severing the last remaining thread between father and son.

Pilly, Gus, Pupi, and me

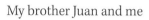
My brother Juan and me

Mom and me

Daddy and me

Me at Video One

Garage where I lived with Chiquis

Chiquis's baby shower

Chiquis, Jacqie,
Mikey, and me

My little soldier Johnny and me

Left: My princes, princesses and me

Below: My beautiful Jenicka wearing her quinceañera dress and me. Thanking God for that special day.

Rosie, Jacqie, Chiquis, Jenicka, and me

With my daughters and my granddaughter Jaylah

At a concert in the Querétaro Fair in Mexico with over 80,000 fans

Chapter 6 -

This is it. This is the most difficult chapter of my life. This is the story which is hardest to tell. The one that I believe both tore me down, and, exalted me. This is experience has been the most traumatic one in my life and therefore, the most difficult to overcome. For days, I've procrastinated and have tried to avoid writing this chapter. However, I know that I cant and I shouldnt. I believe in my heart that this is what God wants me to do. SOMEONE must do it. SOMEONE must come forward and after all ends tell it to it is. SOMEONE must have the courage to let our people know how terribly serious sexual abuse can be to the life of a human being. We must let children know that it can happen to them and that it is not their fault. Mothers must know that there is hope and happiness after much suffering. Someone! let the latin community know that abuse and incest occur more of we want to imagine. ANYONE exposed to it and ANYONE can be a sexual molestor. Yet Someone had to speak up and tell you, first hand, that Sexual abuse has a huge effect on a child's mind and soul. If not dealt with, it can be destroying and everlasting. For one reason or another I am that "someone". This is not only my story. ~~Nor is it the story of only my children and me~~ Nor is it just the story of my sister, my children, and ~~my family~~. It is the story of many prostitutes, drug addicts, criminals and mentally ill patients, ~~whom~~ who were not as fortunate as we were and couldn't deal with the pain and the reality of having been abused as children. This is our story.

It was a hot August Sunday in 1997. "Summertime in the LBC," I thought while driving down the 91 Fwy to Ministerio Logos, the church our family attended in Long Beach. Pastor Tin Mejias had asked ~~us~~ all members of the church to make sure we attended on that particular Sunday. There would be, he promised, a special deliverance of the word of God. He had invited evangelist and evangelist _____ _____ to preach that Sunday afternoon. Many members of my family would be there. ~~I also~~ My children and I would attend wanting desperately to hear the positive promises the Lord had for ~~my~~ us. ~~Children an I was excite~~ I was excited. Little did I know.

After preaching the word the prophet made an alter call. He wanted to ~~pray~~ pray for anyone who had a special need either physically or emotionally. As members of the church came forward for prayer he would look around and call out others whom had not stepped forward. He prayed and profesized to many that afternoon. Some would find jobs, some would be healed of illnesses, some would grow spiritually, some would have to make changes in order to be happier in life. To others he profesized about their marraiges and family situations. Suddenly he sees my sister sitting ~~in one of~~ quietly on one of the church benches. He looked at her, pointed her out, and asked her to come forward. "The Lord has word for you young Lady," he said. "You are special

in the eyes of the lord. He loves you."
Rosie, sixteen at the time, began crying.
He looked at her and said, "No More."
It will be over right now, right here."
The profet had a stern but tender look
on his face. "I demand" he said, "For
all spirit of sexual abuse to exit this
girl's life." I remember being shocked
to hear him. "A spirit of sexual abuse
has surrounded your life since you
were a little girl. It has saddened
and tormented you. You have not been
able to be a normal little girl because
of it. But God tells me to tell you
that it ends here." He said. "Sadness,
no more. Torment, no more. I order these
spirits to exit your life immediately."

I dont know what the rest of our
family thought, but personally I didnt
want to give it much thought. I didnt
want to question my sister. I wouldn't
ask a thing. there was no way I would
make her feel uncomfortable. I was a
firm believer in God's word and knew
that sooner or later whatever my sister
was dealing with would come to light

pirited lipped ~~upset~~ Juan in the Bathroom. He was upset that I was thirty minutes late. "I thought I told you I wanted us to leave at 5pm, Jenni," he said. "I ~~know~~ baby, I'm sorry. I couldn't find anything I liked. I'll be ready in a second." I hurried to begin doing my hair. "If ~~you~~ hadn't been wasting your time on the internet chatting with your fans ~~there~~ we'd be leaving already." His voice noticeably more upset. "I said I would be ready fast, Juan. Don't make me bring up shit that you've done which has really affected our relationship. We both know ~~you're~~ quite good a wasting time doing ~~things you~~ shouldn't do." I was beginning to get irritated. We went back and ~~forth~~ until he threatened to go to ~~the~~ wedding without me. "I dare you, I said. "I dare you to go without me," I watched him drive off as I ~~stood~~ ~~by~~ ~~the~~ looked out the bathroom window.

For days after we didn't speak to each other. No words. No cooking or attending to his needs. No sex. No nothing. I'd sleep in the living room and he'd keep the bed, as he usually did when we had fights. He tried ~~to convince me and make things~~ to make-up on various occasions. When he noticed I wasn't giving in he'd try to get to me through the kids. He never convinced me. I was done. On April 23, 2003 I did it. I filed for divorce and had his sister, ~~Sta~~ Maria, serve him the divorce papers. I wasn't messing around.

For two months we lived like strangers in the same house. Although I was determined to go through with the divorce it hurt me to know it would be over. ~~I did love my husband dearly, I just did~~

I loved him dearly but didn't like him at all anymore. The physical attraction was there but the mental attraction was gone. He had ~~done~~ so many mistakes~~things~~ that, en my openion, lacked mental entelligence. ~~that type~~ ~~of~~ Those mistakes had caused a change of heart in me. ~~I thought~~ now that I had gone ~~as to~~ this far, he would make a change. He didnt. Instead of making the right moves and conducting himself as a respectable man, he made even more mistakes.

My eldest daughter, whom was in ~~her~~ high school at ~~the~~ ~~last year~~ time began hearing rumors that her "dad" had been seen with girls at Hacienda Night Club, in Norco. She'd hear defferent rumors weekly and felt ashamed and embarrased that Juan would dare act the fool at ~~its~~ a place so close to Home.

he was easily identified. I began to feel stupid. The image of a strong woman I had created before my fans and the music industry was being tarnished. In order to maintain my dignity I was going to have to speak up.

On June 31st 2003 I had a radio interview with ThomasRubio a disc jockey at Que Buena 105.5 FM A couple of weeks before I had told him I wasn't ready to speak about it when he mentioned he had heard the news. By now it had gotten out of hand however. ~~During the~~ interview I ~~mentioned~~ clarified that ~~In~~ we had begun divorce proceedings ~~a coupl~~ almost three months ~~before~~ and that ~~Juan~~ technically, Juan was a free man.

That was it. The next day on July 1st I was invited to perform a track I had done with

7

Breaking Away

Espere mucho tiempo pa' ver si cambiabas
Y tú ni me miras.

(I waited so long to see if you'd change.
And you didn't even look at me.)
        —from "Nieves de Enero"

I gained sixty pounds when I was pregnant with Michael, and after I delivered him I was hit with the baby blues (nobody called it postpartum depression back then). When I least expected it, the fights with Trino were back, and they were much worse this time. Once again he belittled me and called me fat. He got heated and jealous over the most minor situations. I was bringing in the most money and bearing the financial responsibility of raising three kids and paying a mortgage, and maybe that made him insecure, so he tried to keep me down. Who knows?

It's crazy how violent, possessive relationships can become so addictive. For so long I kept going back for more, and each time I did,

I somehow thought that I was strengthening our love. It seemed impossible for me to live without the father of my children and the first man in my life. It didn't help much that I was still intent on being like my mother and hanging in there forever. I can't ever be with another man, I thought. My father wouldn't allow it. Yet, over the years, my father came to know how rocky our relationship was. I didn't know it at the time, but Rosie would report back on the abuse she witnessed whenever she slept over. And when we lived in the back house or in the house nearby on Fifty-Fifth Street, the rest of my family would hear our fights. As hard as it was for them, my daddy told my brothers to never get involved in anyone else's relationship and to mind their own business. And so they didn't intervene.

But one day during the early summer of 1992, my father surprised me by not following his own advice. We were sitting at the dining-room table at my parents' house on Ellis Street. Daddy looked at me and asked, "Aren't there any other men in the world, *mija*? Why are you so stuck on this one? Do you not feel worthy of being loved and admired by another fish in the ocean?" I was surprised, but happy to hear him say such words. It meant that if I did someday meet, date, or fall in love with someone else, it would be okay with him. Since he was the boss, it would have to be okay with the rest of my family too. It was on.

I was sick of taking Trino's shit. In August of 1992, he hit me for the last time. I was too tired to fight back. Instead, I called the cops and put his ass in jail. This time we were over for good. Something in me finally said, "No more."

While he was in jail, I began going out with friends. I was twenty-three and had never been to a club, aside from the singing competitions I'd gone to with my father. I hardly went out at all. When you get pregnant at fifteen, that kind of thing falls by the wayside. And when you are married to a man like Trino, forget about it. Now that

I no longer had him running my life, I could make up for a bit of lost time. I learned how to have fun, drink, and let loose. I enjoyed being able to dance again like when I was young and carefree at backyard barbecues or in my parents' bedroom.

Wherever I went, music was always blasting and I was always singing along. But I had not set foot on a stage to sing since I was eleven years old and had forgotten the words at the singing competition. One night when we were at El Rancho Grande, a nightclub in Carson, a friend said, "I dare you to go up there and sing." Then another friend said, "Naw, she's not down." That's all I needed to hear, and they knew it. I walked onstage and told the norteño group that was playing that I wanted to sing "Nieves de Enero." Chalino Sánchez had passed away during that year, and the track was popular at the time. I stood in front of the crowd, and as soon as the first words came out of my mouth, I was overwhelmed by so many emotions. I was reminded how much I loved the feeling of being onstage. I was reminded that I had a voice. When I was finished, the entire club started to clap and cheer. I felt as if I could fly.

It had been twelve years since the day in 1980 when I'd told my father I would never touch a microphone again, but he had been right, that one day I would end up onstage again without his pushing or persuading me. All it took was a dare. After that night I decided to record a complete album for my father as a birthday gift. I knew how much it would mean to him, and I had fun doing it. I went into a studio and sang under the name Jenni "La Güera Rivera" Rivera. The title of the album was *Somos Rivera*. I never thought anyone would hear it besides my dad, but he fell in love with it and asked me if he could promote it under his record label, Cintas Acuario.

"Do whatever you want with it," I told him. "It's yours. But if you are going to promote it, use the name Jenni and spell it with an *i*."

I never thought anything would come of it, but that album was what launched my recording career. It's not as if I were an overnight success, but I got some good feedback and it made me think that maybe my father was right. Maybe I did have a future in this? But as soon as I asked the question, I was knocked back down again.

In 1994, I got a small gig in Encinitas near San Diego to open for another singer, who was one of my father's artists. I had to pay for gas, food, and a wardrobe out of my own pocket, and I was making only $300. As I was walking to the bathroom, I heard a friend of my dad's talking to the manager who had hired me. We were outside and I was walking on grass, so they didn't hear me approaching. Dad's friend said, "Who did you invite to open?"

"I got this new girl, Jenni Rivera," the manager told him.

"Why did you invite her? She can't sing. She's ugly. She has a bad attitude."

I was hurt and I was pissed. My father produced this man's daughter's music, and now here he was talking crap about me to other people in the industry. I went onstage not long after that and sang my heart out, trying to prove to myself, more than anyone else, that I belonged on a stage. But I wasn't so sure. All I wanted was to get home to my kids. As soon as I was done, I went to the manager to ask him for my $300.

"Oh, I'll pay you," he said, "after you have sex with me."

I was horrified and heated, but could do little. I told that asshole right off and I walked out of there without getting paid. When I got home, I told my dad, "I am never singing again. This industry is too ugly. I'm not putting myself through this crap. I can make more money in real estate anyway."

"I understand, *mija*," he responded. "But please do me one more favor. Record one more album. I already have a lot of the songs, I have the lyrics. Just one more."

I could never say no to my father. I recorded that second album, and it got the attention of some people at Balboa Records, and I signed on to do a third album with them, which I titled *La Maestra*.

When Trino found out, he started to come around the house and the real estate office trying to persuade me to give our relationship another chance. But I didn't budge. No way was I going down that road again. I was done for good. When I said my final no to Trino, he responded with words I will never forget: "You don't want to get back together with me although we have three kids? You think you are going to make it in that stupid singing career? Listen to me, you're never going to make it as an artist. You sound too much like Graciela Beltrán, anyway. You'll always be compared to her and will never be taken seriously. You need to stop with your dumbass dreams." He said it with such passion, and a part of me wanted to tell him that he was the dumbass, but a part of me worried that he might be right.

Although I enjoyed making Trino think otherwise, I wasn't seriously pursuing a career in music because half the time I wasn't even getting paid. When I had my first gig outside of California, one of my brothers came with me. It was in Washington, DC, and we flew in a day early to see the city.

The night of my gig I was supposed to be paid a few thousand dollars, but at the end of the night the manager who had hired me refused to pay. He said his business partner never gave him the money. My brother was ready to beat his ass, but I told him that instead we should have the manager drive us to the business partner's house and ask for the money. So we did just that, but the partner didn't have it either. So we made the manager take a bat to his partner's car. Then we drove the manager to the park across the street from the White House and made him strip down naked. My brother took his car keys and chucked them deep into the park. We left him there, naked, searching for his car keys in the light of the White House. Just so he knew you don't fuck with the Riveras.

Breaking away from the heavy chains that attached me to Trino was one of the smartest moves I ever made. It was also one of the hardest. I truly loved him, but I loved my children more and I could not go back to him again.

About a year after Trino and I separated, the real estate market took a negative turn once more. Meanwhile, the album I had recorded for Balboa Records was going nowhere fast because they refused to promote it. I was in deep shit and struggling to keep up the house payments while supporting the kids on my own, since Trino refused to help financially. I was forced to put my pride on the shelf and go on welfare, which was demoralizing.

One month I couldn't pay the water bill, so I told the kids they could only use the restroom at school. But one day Chiquis forgot. She pooped in the house and couldn't flush it. I saw her dart out of the bathroom and down the hallway. I knew something was up. I walked toward the bathroom, where I found Jacqie eating her sister's poop. She was covered in it. The hairbrush was covered in it. It was smeared across the bathroom tiles. I screamed in horror. I had no way of cleaning her up, and she just kept saying, "I'm sorry, Mommy. I'm sorry." I couldn't help but laugh. I threw away her clothes, the brush, and the bathroom towels, and then washed Jacqie with the neighbor's hose.

Although times were difficult for me economically, emotionally I was much more stable. I was free from Trino's control, from his constant judgment and put-downs, his narrow-mindedness, and his volatile temper. Then the universe threw me a bone and the real estate market picked back up, even stronger than before. I went from being on welfare to making as much as $24,000 a month. For the first time in a long time I felt as if I could breathe again.

On February 25, 1995, I went out with a friend to El Farallon. Marisela, Chalino Sánchez's widow, had become a close friend after his death. We became each other's confidantes and shoulders to cry on when we needed support. Just as I had been there for her after Chalino's death, she wanted to be there for me during my hardships. My brother Juan, who was sixteen years old at the time, had been arrested and convicted for the attempted sale and transportation of narcotics. Marisela knew my brother was my angel baby. He was my "roll dog." I'd sneak him into the clubs and bars and anywhere I went to have fun. He was my homey, my Angel Face, and my protector. When Trino came around to my house on Fifty-Fifth Street to try to beat me up, I would call Juan. He would run the three blocks from my parents' house to my house with a baseball bat in his hand. He'd defend me and scare Trino away. He would tie a naked man to a tree to defend my honor.

I was devastated that I wouldn't see Juan for six months while he did time at Camp Mendenhall at Lake Hughes. I broke down when I heard the news from my sobbing mother. Marisela wanted to make sure that I didn't stay locked up in the house crying, so that night she took me out to see El Puma de Sinaloa, my favorite local artist, who would be performing at El Farallon.

I still wasn't giving my music my full attention because the money was so unstable and the industry was so unreliable. From the time I was a child, I have been a businesswoman before all else. I was making a great living in real estate. I had purchased a home in Compton on Aprilia Avenue, where I lived with my three children, and I didn't have to worry about whether I was going to be able to pay the water bill anymore. I wasn't about to give all that up and fall at the mercy of a shady, often cruel industry. Not until that shady, often cruel industry offered to promote me and pay up. So even though Marisela and many others believed in me and tried to get me to focus on my singing, I just couldn't do it. It was still a secondary concern.

However, a *corrido* I wrote called "La Chacalosa" had earned me a special underground following with a certain group in LA. The lyrics told the story of a drug-trafficking female who was "making it big in the business." At the time the Los Angeles area had many popular drug dealers. My *corrido* appealed to them, and many of these mafiosos knew who I was and respected me. They would see Marisela and me around the clubs and make sure we were taken care of. That night one dealer insisted that I sing "La Chacalosa" for him. He had the power to stop the DJ and order the live norteño group to play whatever he wanted to hear. He came to our table and said, "Go up there and sing my *corrido*, girl. I'll pay you whatever you want." Of course, I wasn't going to charge the man a dime.

"Go for it," Marisela told me with an approving look.

I went onstage with El Vampiro y Sus Fantasmas and they began to play "La Chacalosa." Halfway through the song, a tall dark handsome man came onstage with a friend and asked the photographer of the club to take a Polaroid picture of all three of us while I was performing. Because I was used to the attention from fans, I didn't make much of it.

Marisela and I left the club with the rest of the VIP clients at two thirty in the morning. We walked out to the parking lot, where only a few cars were left. As we walked toward my Toyota Camry, we noticed two men walking in our direction. When they got closer, I realized one of them was the handsome guy who had taken a picture with me and one of his friends.

"Hi, Jenni." The man introduced himself as Juan.

We talked for a bit, and then they asked us to a late dinner at Las

Playas, a twenty-four-hour restaurant in Bell. Marisela was cautious and immediately responded that we couldn't.

"Vamonos, *güera*," she whispered to me. "We don't know them. It's getting late anyway."

"Thanks, but we can't," I told Juan. "It was nice meeting you."

He wouldn't take his eyes off me. "Then give me your autograph and your phone number."

I gave him both.

8

Grant Me the Serenity

Why should I keep loving you,
When I know that you're not true?
> —from "Wasted Days and Wasted Nights"

Juan and I began to date no more than a week after we first met. I was crazy about him from the start. He was so handsome, sweet, and attentive. By August, just five months later, we moved in together. Or rather, he moved into my house in Compton. Looking back, I don't know what the hell I was thinking. It could have, and should have, happened differently. I could have asked him to leave when he spent more than three nights at my house, but I didn't say anything. I couldn't hear the roaring of the motor as my new roller-coaster ride headed toward destruction. I was in love. And love makes you stupid.

The relationship between Juan and me was not as difficult and dramatic as my relationship with Trino. It was, however, equally addictive. That we didn't have as many arguments and disagreements made it easier to have fun, and from the beginning we spent a lot of time together. Our regular outings were to the movies (I hadn't been to a movie since I got pregnant with my first daughter) and to various nightclubs. We both loved to dance and enjoyed going to El Merca-dito in Los Angeles to listen to the live mariachi bands and take part in Corona-beer-drinking contests. We had something else in common, something important: a love for baseball. Unlike Trino, Juan played sports and was a catcher on his baseball team. The kids and I were regulars at his weekend games. Because we shared so many equal interests, and because I didn't act like a normal girl, he said it was easy for him to fall in love with me. "You don't bore me," he'd say. "It's like kicking it with another one of the guys." I felt just the same about him.

I think it's normal (or at least I hope it is) to be more naive and vulnerable when you are younger. It's easy to fall in love with someone for the person's looks without considering whether the person has other important qualities. That's what happened to me with Juan. I didn't care that he wasn't as ambitious as I was, or that he had no interest in growing spiritually or morally. I didn't care that, at twenty-three years old, he had fathered three children with three different women, and that he didn't support any of them financially and would only, occasionally, visit one of them. I didn't question how at the beginning of our relationship he asked me to charge a set of Dayton rims for the Grand Marquis he drove. I never questioned how he didn't offer to repay me for them. In fact, as I sank deeper into debt and struggled to sell real estate, I included those rims and the credit card in my Chapter 11 bankruptcy file. Call me dumb. Call me crazy. Call me whatever you want. I know. I was a blind ding-dong, enjoying "true love" to the fullest. I couldn't see a thing.

Despite his many defects, Juan did have valuable virtues. He was respectful to my family and kids. He wanted to maintain a good relationship with my loved ones. He wasn't possessive or jealous like my ex-husband and wouldn't question or interrogate me every time I left the house. He would push me to do better. He thought I was intelligent and had my back if I wanted to continue my education. He gave me enough space to go out in the field to find real estate clients. He believed in my talent, and although I still didn't take my singing career seriously, he knew that if I tried, I would one day make it. "My girl will be the best in her genre," he'd tell me and his family. Also unlike in the case of Trino, I had a beautiful relationship with Juan's family. He knew I loved him and I knew he loved me too. With all this in mind, I wanted to stay with him forever. I was certain that this relationship was going to work.

However, it wasn't always so fine and dandy. Sure, it was great at the beginning, but things took a turn for the worse when I least expected it. During January 1996, with the funds I had saved after a few closed sales, I was able to put a down payment on an FHA loan for a house on Keene Avenue in Compton. Because I had filed for bankruptcy in 1995, I couldn't purchase it under my name; therefore both the loan and the title were under Juan's name. I paid for the house, but he was the legal owner. I trusted my man. What a dumbass.

Our fights were never as violent and physical as my fights with Trino, but we did have our mini-matches. There would be some pushing and shoving here and there. If I recall correctly, it was February 16, 1996, a weekend night. The kids were visiting with Trino and his new girlfriend, Dora, as they did every weekend. Juan and I had an argument about something so minor I can't even remember what it was. To cool off, I went shopping at the Target in Carson for a couple of hours. When I came home, he was gone.

Our bedroom smelled of his cologne and I noticed the iron was out. That night we were supposed to go to his friend's wedding together. I couldn't believe he had left without me. I sat home and waited. Midnight came around. Then 1:00 a.m. Then 2:00 a.m. He still wasn't back. I was furious and plotted a way to get back at him. Finally, at 2:30

in the morning, his car pulled into the driveway. I was hiding by the side of the house. As soon as I heard the motor turn off, I jumped out and screamed, "Surprise!" With all my strength I threw a brick straight toward the front windshield of his Grand Marquis. As soon as I saw it crack into pieces, I ran at top speed back into the house. I could hear him swearing up a storm as I ran from the front yard, through the living room, and toward our bedroom. I didn't make it to my destination. My race to safety came to a stop on the floor in the hallway. We pushed, pulled, and shoved each other. I tore his trademark chain off his neck. That was like cutting off one of his balls! In the end, he pushed me a little too hard, and because I refused to ever again take any physical abuse from anyone, I called the Compton police.

When the cops arrived, I was sitting in the living room. By then Juan was a lot calmer and could reason better than I could. The police officers asked him to leave to make sure another confrontation would be avoided.

"I can't," Juan told him. "I've been drinking."

"Then you leave me with no other option," the officer said. "We will have to arrest you."

"If you arrest me, you have to arrest her too," Juan told him as he showed off the scratch marks I had left on his chest.

The officer turned to me. "Did you do that, ma'am?"

"I sure as hell did," I answered, putting my wrists together so he could snap the handcuffs on me.

Juan looked at me. "Jenni, stop. We can still drop the charges. Be smart."

"Naw, fool," I responded. "We're going to jail."

They drove us in separate police cars. I couldn't believe this was really happening. There I was in the back of a police car as the officers stopped by the drive-through of the doughnut shop on Rosecrans and Central. Then they took me to the Compton jail. I sat on the cold, hard floor wondering what the hell I had been thinking. The cops interviewed us and tried to mediate the situation. That's when I heard Juan say, "Well, the house is mine. It is not your house." This was the first sign of his being a greedy asshole and was a red flag as to what was to come. I was so fucking pissed at him and even more pissed at myself.

I called my brother Juan from jail that night. Although I'd probably be released in the next few days, Juan begged my parents to bail me out. He couldn't bear his sister spending time in jail. Since the O. J. Simpson case, a major change had occurred in the laws regarding domestic violence. Bail amounts were much higher. My parents had to come up with 10 percent of $50,000, plus they put up the title to their house as collateral. Of course I paid my parents the $5,000 back as soon as I could. That's what I got for being a stupid shit.

Eventually, Juan and I dropped all charges against each other. I realized that, as in so many incidents before and after, I was at fault. I wasn't perfect. One of the great things about Juan was that he would forgive and forget easily. We vowed to try harder and to make it work for the sake of our love and the kids. Juan told me that despite our differences and problems, he never wanted to see me with someone else.

Our efforts worked for a while, until he was arrested and convicted for immigrant smuggling on August 1 of that same year. During his seven months in prison he was transferred from El Centro, California, to Arizona, to Oklahoma, and finally to a correctional facility in Big Spring, Texas. I wanted to make sure I did whatever I could to make those seven months as bearable as possible for him. I loved him. I had to be his gangsta bitch and have his back. During Thanksgiving weekend I bought a plane ticket and flew to Texas to see him. I rented a car, drove in the pouring rain, and got lost on my way to Big Spring. I didn't care. The only thing on my mind was to surprise him and let him know how much I loved him. I rented a hotel room for the weekend and visited him each day. We talked about what we were going to do when he got out, how we both were going to be better for each other and for ourselves. I told him about how I drove around to the different radio stations to deliver a master copy of "La Chacalosa" to them, but none of them was playing it because I wouldn't pay off the disc jockeys. He told me not to worry, that that I was going to be a big star one day. He was sure of it.

Fast-forward two months, to me sitting on the pavement on a street in Compton. Waiting for the three men in the white sports car to drive away. Feeling the pain and shame of what had just happened to me. Hearing the green-eyed monster hissing, "Aren't you El Cinco's lady?" and "Leave me the fuck alone," over and over.

I sat on that pavement long after I saw their taillights disappear. I wanted to make sure they were really gone. Once I felt that they were never coming back, I lifted myself off the curb and walked over to my car to get myself home.

That night I couldn't sleep. I sat there in the darkness, all alone, shattered inside. I didn't feel like the same Jenni anymore. Ever since I was a little girl, I was a fighter. I could go toe-to-toe with any of the boys from the neighborhood. But my will had been taken away. I was no longer the tough, brave, invincible girl my father and brothers had raised. I had lost my first fight.

A mixture of fear, sadness, hatred, and deep shame took over me. I relived the trauma in my head over and over, wondering what I could have done differently. Why did I get out of the car? Why hadn't I been smart enough to memorize their plates? Why didn't I pull into the gas station on Central Avenue and scream for help? Why didn't I kick them in the balls as my brothers had taught me? I decided I wouldn't tell anyone. I wouldn't call the cops. I wouldn't worry my parents or any of my family members. I wouldn't dare tell my kids. Instead, I kept it inside and fell into a deep depression, all on my own. I didn't want anyone to know that I was no longer the intelligent warrior my father was so proud of. That Jenni was gone forever. She had disappeared in the back of that white sports car.

Juan was released three weeks later, on February 14, 1997. I picked him up around 8:00 p.m. at LAX. I tried my best to hide that I was going through a difficult time. I had been depressed and deeply suffering since the night of the rape. Juan would walk into our bedroom to find me crying inconsolably. "You don't love me anymore, do you?" he'd say. "You don't seem happy that I'm back home."

"Please be patient with me right now, babe. I need you at this time. I do love you very much. More than you can imagine."

What he couldn't imagine was that I was not the same woman I had been when he first went to jail. He couldn't imagine how weak my mind was or the trauma I had endured. Holding each other that night, we cried until we fell asleep.

After a few days, because I felt that it was driving me crazy, I told him what had happened. For years I never told anyone else. Confiding in Juan felt good inside. He embraced me and so badly wanted to help me feel better. I couldn't help but wonder if he knew who I was talking about when I described the man with the green eyes who hissed, "Aren't you El Cinco's lady?" But Juan didn't say a word.

Soon Juan began a job at Fairchild Fasteners in Torrance. My brother Gus worked there and recommended Juan for a high-paying position. However, since Juan was an alien resident who had committed a serious felony, proceedings for his deportation also began. After analyzing every other option, the attorney we hired advised us that the only way for Juan to avoid deportation would be if he married a US citizen. So what did I do? Right.

We were married in a civil ceremony at Norwalk City Hall on June 9, 1997. I was with my groom, my three children, and four months pregnant with my fourth child. Juan was excited that we were having a baby. He thought a baby would keep us together. I was not as happy. I thought this would put a halt to the minimal underground success I had attained with my song "Las Malandrinas." People in the industry assured me that it was a jumping-off point, but then there I went and got pregnant again. Though I wasn't exactly thrilled about having another baby, I was happy that we were finally experiencing some stability in our relationship.

A major part of this newfound peace was due to our attending church regularly. We were growing both spiritually and emotionally. I felt that the bond between us was becoming stronger and stronger. I was happy I had married him, although it wasn't for all the right reasons nor was it under the best of circumstances. I didn't get the wedding I had always dreamed of, but we planned for one in the near future. Our love, we felt, deserved to be celebrated in a religious ceremony. We needed God's blessing.

In the months after we married, we were faithful visitors at the Wednesday, Friday, and Sunday services at Ministerio Logos, a Baptist church where my brother Pete was assistant pastor. Pete and Pastor Mejias taught the Word in a way it had never been taught to me before. My reason for living was a lot clearer, as was my spirituality. I felt that for once in my life I had found peace. I was good. God was good. I learned that He works in mysterious ways to show us His goodness.

On an unbearably hot Sunday in August of that year, I was headed down the 91 freeway toward our church. Pastor Tin Mejias had asked all the parishioners to make sure we attended on that particular Sunday. He had invited a prophet, Noe Sierra, to preach and deliver the Word of God. Many members of my family were there. My children and I sat in the pew, desperately wanting to hear the positive promises the Lord had for us. I was excited. Little did I know.

God spoke through him in a powerful and surprising way. He began calling members and visitors of the church up to the altar. He'd say a special prayer for everyone he called forward. He prophesied to many that afternoon. Some would find jobs, some would be healed of illnesses, some would grow spiritually, some would have to make changes to be happier in life . . . Suddenly, he saw Rosie, who was then sixteen, sitting quietly on one of the church pews. He looked at her, pointed her out, and asked her to come forward.

"The Lord has Word for you, young lady," he said. "He wants me to tell you that you are special to Him. He loves you." Rosie began to cry. He looked at her. "No more. It will be over right now, right here." The prophet had a stern but tender look on his face. "At this moment all chains of sadness and depression shall be broken. You will no longer be tied down by those spirits. Spirit of sexual abuse, exit her life!" I stared in shock. "A spirit of sexual abuse has surrounded your life since you were a little girl. It has saddened and tormented you. You have not been able to be a normal little girl because of it. But God tells me to tell you that it ends here. Sadness, no more. Torment, no more."

I was numb, but knew that it truly was the Lord who spoke through the prophet on that unforgettable Sunday morning.

I don't know what the rest our family thought that day, but I didn't want to put my sister in an uncomfortable position. I wouldn't ask her about what the prophet had said. I knew that sooner or later whatever she was dealing with would come to light. I prayed for her soul that night. I asked God to let me help in any way I could. I asked Him to bless the sister I loved so much. I repeated the prayer I had learned at the rehab center when I was younger: "Dear God, grant me the serenity to accept the things I cannot change, the courage to change the things I can, and the wisdom to know the difference."

9

God Never Gives Us More Than We Can Handle

Through many dangers, toils and snares,
I have already come;
'Tis grace hath brought me safe thus far,
And grace will lead me home.

—from "Amazing Grace"

"*He knows our weaknesses,* but He also knows our strengths. If we are going through difficult experiences, trials, or tribulations, it is because God knows we are strong enough to deal with them. He knows we can learn from the experience and hopefully be able to help others who may be experiencing the same problem. God never gives us more than we can handle." My pastor's preaching was resounding in my mind on that gloomy September 23, 1997. Pastor Tin had taught me so much about the Word of God and how to apply His teachings to my own life.

God is good, I thought as I stood in front of the glass door at my brother's office building on Market Street. I was seven months pregnant and didn't feel like getting all dressed up for work at the Century 21 office I was working out of in those days. At Pete's office I could dress more kicked back and wait for the kids to get out of school, which was right down the street. God knows everything, I thought as I rubbed my tummy, feeling my baby kick. Just at that moment I saw Rosie walk down the street toward the office. My beautiful sister, I thought. I loved her so much. Her existence was such a blessing to my life. I could see her hair blowing in the wind as she squinted her eyes because of the sunlight. She looked to be deep in thought about something.

By the time Rosie walked into the office I was sitting at my desk drinking water, trying to make it to the sixty-four ounces that my gynecologist insisted I drink each day. When Rosie sat in the chair across from me, I sensed something was off. "What's up, Sister? How was school today?" She sat quietly. She seemed sad as she stared down at the floor. With Rosie you never knew how she was feeling on any given day. She was so quiet sometimes, and she kept to herself.

"Rosie, what's wrong? I feel like you have something to say but you're scared to tell me." I looked her straight in her beautiful, big brown eyes. "You know you can tell me anything. You can always trust me. I will never judge you." She still didn't speak. "Are you holding back on telling me something because I am pregnant? Whatever it is, I can take it, Rosie." She began crying and my heart broke. "I can take it, Rosie," I said again as the tears rolled down her face.

"Yes, I have something to tell you," she said. "For many years I have wanted to tell you but I couldn't." She was sobbing.

"Yes?" I asked, though I was scared to hear whatever was coming.

"Since I was seven years old, I was sexually abused. It stopped when I was eleven, but I never had the courage to tell you."

My body went numb. I don't know if my heart started beating faster or if it stopped beating altogether. "By who? Who did it?"

She brought her hands to her face. She wouldn't respond.

"Do I know this person?"

She nodded her head yes.

I started to name people and finally she stopped me and said, "Trino."

"How? When? Where?" I sobbed. Rosie seemed unready to tell me all the details, but I had no doubt that he had done it. The son of a bitch had committed the unforgivable.

How could he do this to my sister? He knew how much I loved her. He knew how much she meant to me. Why would he do this?

Rosie said, "Wait. There is more." I looked at her face and she said, "Where is Chiquis?"

I could not breathe. I knew what that meant. I thought my heart could not break any more until that moment. My two babies. How could he have done this to my two baby dolls?

I dropped to my knees and screamed without pause. I screamed so loud that my parents heard me from the offices of their record label across the street, they heard me at the apartments next door, and all throughout the building. Rosie was terrified of my reaction. She ran outside to meet everyone who had run across the street to see what had happened to me. I ran after her. Then I ran back in the office and back out. I didn't know what to do. Ramona, my brother Pete's wife, was the first one on the scene. My brother Lupillo followed her, and then my parents and the employees at the record label and the neighbors at the grocery store next door. I couldn't speak. It was too much for me to handle. The pain was unbearable. The tough girl I had been all my life was breaking into pieces. I needed more than valor and bravery. I needed direction.

"God. Dear Lord, please help me," I prayed. "I need you. Please show me what to do. Take this pain from me. I can't handle this alone. Please don't abandon me now." I was shaking, crying, and dying inside.

Chiquis was at the library, and I sent my sister-in-law Brenda to go get her. Chiquis walked into the office and she seemed to know what was going on right away. She saw the tears. She saw the commotion. I asked everyone to leave the room. I needed to be alone with my daughter. She was only twelve years old, but she was mature beyond her years. She sat in the same chair Rosie had sat in, knowing something was terribly wrong. I sat at my desk across from her.

"I need you to tell me the truth," I told her.

"This is about my daddy, right? It's about what he does to me." She spoke in a soft voice; her little sneakers were shaking on the ground.

I tried to be strong for her. Though I was broken inside, I couldn't show my baby. "Yes. Don't be scared. Mommy will understand." She was so brave as she told me the hell she had been living through since she was seven years old. I hugged my daughter close and kept repeating to her, "Mama is going to fix it. Mama is going to make it okay."

Both Chiquis and Rosie told me in detail when, where, how much, how often, and since when it had been happening. Everything. They both knew all about sex. Trino had done it all. He had taken their innocence since the ages of seven and eight. It had gone on for four years each. Where was I? Why hadn't I figured it out? Why hadn't they ever told me?

Suddenly my sadness and pain turned to anger. I ran out of the office looking for my brothers. I wanted to kill Trino that very day. I wanted to beat him with a baseball bat. Lupillo and Juan agreed with me that we should get rid of him ourselves, but Pete, Gus, and our parents told us that was the worst thing we could do.

Ramona prayed for us to understand that we had to file a police report. We had to do things right. I was too filled with anger and thoughts of revenge. Fuck the cops. I was going to kill that sick fuck myself. I threw a baseball bat in the trunk of my car. I was on a mission, but then my father pleaded with me not to leave.

"I don't want any of my children incarcerated for homicide," he said. "That's not in my plans for my family's life. We have to be civilized and allow this to be dealt with legally. The police will take care of him."

My mother echoed his thoughts. "Your father is right. The vengeance is not yours. It is God's. He will take care of it. Please don't make this worse than it already is. We cannot suffer more tragedy."

My parents' tears and visible pain held me back.

We went down to the station to file a police report. I sat in the room with Rosie and then with Chiquis as they told the officers, in detail, what Trino had done to them. It was horrific to listen to, but I had to be strong for them. I had to show them that they were safe and they needed to tell as much as they could remember. Trino had started with Rosie one night after he and I got in a huge fight. After that Trino would come for her every time we had a fight. It was as though he was trying to get back at me through my beloved sister. I couldn't breathe thinking back on all the fights we had through the years and the fear Rosie must have been feeling each time. The guilt was crushing me. Trino had told Rosie that he would kill me and our whole family if she ever told anyone, so she stayed quiet. He stopped with her once she developed pubic hair, which apparently grossed him out, she said. And that's when he started on Chiquis, or so we thought. Chiquis could remember it starting at seven, but afterward I took the girls for physical examinations and the evidence suggested that he had molested her as early as two years old. I had my second daughter, Jacqie, examined as well, and there was the same evidence, though thankfully Jacqie had no recollection of any abuse. I truly believe that God protected her from the trauma.

When we got back to our house in Compton, Chiquis told me why she'd never confessed what had been happening to her. "I knew you would kill him. I know you, Mom. Then I wouldn't have a mommy or a daddy. He would be dead and you would be in jail. I learned to forgive my daddy for what he would do to me. Pastor Tin would say that God wants us to forgive. That's what I learned from church, Mommy."

I didn't know how to respond. I didn't know what was right or what was wrong. I was going crazy.

That night my insanity became even more intense. The kids and Juan were all asleep, but I was wide awake at 3:00 a.m., sitting on the couch in front of the TV, holding a butcher knife in my hand. I wanted to kill him or myself that night. I didn't want to live anymore. What was the use? The domestic violence. The difficulties of living on welfare and the constant struggles. The rape. Now this. How could all of this happen in one lifetime? How could this be happening to me and my family? This was the kind of stuff I had watched on *The Cristina Show* or *Oprah*, but I had never expected to live it myself. I didn't know how to overcome this. I didn't know if I could.

I cried like a baby that night and many nights to come. Where was God? Why did He allow this to happen? I thought He never gave us more than we could handle? How did He expect me to handle this? What could I possibly learn from such a horrifying experience? What was the lesson behind it?

I didn't even want to know the answers to my questions. I just wanted the pain to go away. I wanted to take my life. But God had other plans for me. He did not let me go that night. He gave me the strength to move forward, slowly, with a heavy heart and heavy soul.

Every time Trino was supposed to take the kids, I would make up some excuse so I could have the time to press formal charges. After a few weeks Trino caught on, disappeared, and became a fugitive from the law.

I wouldn't lay eyes on Trino again until nine years later, but my brothers never ceased to be on the lookout for him. My brothers know everyone underground. People would say to them, "Trino is going to be at this party on this day and at this place." One night we all went to a house in Long Beach where Trino was supposed to be. My brothers were all outside waiting for him. I was nervous. Part of me didn't want him to show up because I knew my brother Juan would kill him. Trino was always afraid of Juan. Though he was the youngest Rivera, he was also the biggest and the toughest. When it comes to protecting his family, he does not hold back. We waited for a while but Trino didn't show up. That probably saved Trino's life and saved Juan from being put behind bars.

Another time I was having a barbecue and Lupe was late. We were calling him, but there was no answer. Finally Lupe got to my house, flustered and out of breath. He had seen Trino on the freeway. Lupe started chasing after Trino in his car. For a good thirty minutes they were on a high-speed chase on the freeway before Lupe lost Trino. We knew Trino was in the area, but he had once again escaped.

I can say that when I found out what Trino had been doing to my babies, everything changed for me. My joy, my motherly dignity, my will to live, were ripped away from me. Though I had experienced difficulties in my life previously, I found out then what true suffering meant. Every day, every minute, every second hurt. The pain and trauma of that time is indescribable.

As a result of my stress and mental exhaustion, our baby girl, Jenicka Priscilla López, was born a few weeks early, on October 3, 1997. I had once prayed for a child who looked like me, and my prayer was answered with Jenicka. The second people saw her they said, "She's your twin!" (And they still do.) She was so perfect, so sweet, and so easygoing. From the time she was an infant I called her Shaniqua.

Don't ask me why. I gave all of my kids (and anyone else close to me) crazy nicknames that make sense only to me. Jenicka got the most: Shaniqua, Shanisse, Chantilly Lace, and Ebatanisha Washington.

I tried my best to be a happy mother to my newborn girl and my older children. I pushed myself to continue being a devoted wife to my new husband. I still sold real estate and worked part-time at my father's record label just as I did when I was pregnant. I cleaned the house and woke up at 4:00 a.m. to cook my husband's breakfast and lunch for the day before he left for work at 5:00 a.m. I tended to my husband's needs as best I could. I wanted him to be proud of me. I needed his love and support more than ever before, and I didn't want to fail as a wife once again.

Unfortunately, by the time November came around, only a month after Jenicka was born, something did not feel right. Juan wasn't as attentive or caring toward me. He seemed distant and began acting weird. He wasn't as happy to spend time with me as he was before. Making our relationship work was no longer his priority and focus. At first, I wanted to shrug it off and act as if I hadn't noticed the changes. I continued to be affectionate toward him although he wasn't affectionate in return. I feared that he would stop loving me. I cried on my knees in desperation as I prayed to God every night: "Please, God, not that. I can't go through this right now. Please make him love me like he did before."

We began fighting about everything. Everything I did bothered him. From the words I said, to going to church, to the music I listened to. He didn't like me playing Tupac or Biggie when he was around. I would change it to something more romantic, such as Sade or Kenny G, but that would only make things worse. We had to listen to the shit he wanted to play. The cooking wasn't good enough anymore. The sink wasn't clean enough. The kids weren't quiet enough. I wasn't good enough either.

One night the kids and I were sitting in the living room of our Compton home watching the Grammys. Juan wasn't there. He had been spending a lot of time out of the house, and I had started to wonder whether he was cheating on me. He'd go to work early, nicely dressed and smelling good. But Juan has always taken care of himself, I told myself. And he loved me. And he knew how much I was going through. He wouldn't dare put me through more. I was dealing with Trino and the girls. We had just had a baby, and we had gotten married to save him from deportation. All of these thoughts were going through my head as I was watching the winners walk to the podium to give their thank-you speeches.

"Mommy," my eight-year-old, Jacqie, shouted. "You're not listening, are you?"

"What? I am."

"I just asked you why you don't sing anymore. You can win a Gammy one day," she said in her innocent little voice.

"Yeah, Mommy," Chiquis seconded her. "Why don't you sing again? You can win a Grammy, or at least be nominated for one."

My poor babies, I thought. If they only knew how difficult and ugly the music industry was. How hard it was to be a female artist in my genre. More than that, if only they knew the real reason I had stopped singing was because my spirit had been so crushed the night I had been raped. I would never tell them the truth. They had more vision and belief in me than anyone else I had met during the time I was singing and recording. They had more vision than their own mother. My kids were dreamers. And that night their dreams lit a spark, a fire in my soul. A few days later, when my dad asked me to record another CD for him, I decided to give it another try. At the very least, as my father always said, I could just record the *corrido* album he so badly yearned for.

In June of 1998 my father called me into his office at La Musica del

Pueblo, one of our family record stores on Pacific Avenue in Huntington Park. But he didn't want to talk music this time. He told me he
had heard from someone that Juan was messing around with quite
a few people at work. Gus knew, but he did not have the guts to tell
me. But my father couldn't bear his daughter being made a fool of and
couldn't hold it in any longer.

"I'm not telling you what to do, *mija*," he said. "That's totally up
to you. You know I've never butted into your relationships, but I
don't think it's right. Especially considering everything you've been
through, especially in this past year, and everything you did for him
when he was locked up. Everyone is talking about it where he works.
You need to make a decision and fix this shit."

I could feel my heart breaking, but I didn't want to show that to
my father. I told him, "I will handle it, Daddy. Don't worry. I will take
care of this motherfucker." As soon as I uttered those words, I felt
myself turn from sad to furious. I stomped out the back door of the
record store. How could Juan do this to me? I asked myself. I loved
him! I was there for him when he was in jail. I had even made his
child-support payments during that time. I married him to save his
ass from deportation. How could he do this to me after I had gone
through so much pain?

As much as I wanted to, I decided not to kill him. It was what I
always thought I would do if a man cheated on me. I knew that if I
confronted him about it and screamed, fought, or cried, it wouldn't
do anything. I had to find a way to really get back at him. As I drove
back to Compton, I thought and thought about what move I would
make. Marisela's CD was playing in the car stereo as I went over op-
tions in my head.

I decided not to say a word. Instead, I came up with a plan. First
and foremost, I would make the fucker fall in love with me again. I
just needed two months.

I hired a private investigator. He videotaped various days of Juan's adventures with the *putas* at work. I found out which motels they would go to. I learned that he would throw away the lunches I'd prepared for him at 4:00 a.m. and go out to lunch with the hoes instead. *"Qué pendeja soy,"* I said to myself.

That summer was sad and emotionally draining for me. All the time my husband was cheating, Gus, my loving brother, the one who'd taught me to defend myself, the one who always called me beautiful, had been aware of what was going on and never told me. It had been going on for months and he said he couldn't find a way to tell me. He too was from the hood and said that he had learned that a man should not rat on another man. He said he wasn't and would never be a little ratting bitch. He loved and adored me and didn't want to hurt me with the knowledge of Juan's infidelity, so he opted to not mention it. I didn't understand his point of view. I was hurt. Gus and I stopped speaking for eight months and ten days. It was painful and it killed me inside to be at family reunions, and we wouldn't cross words with each other. We wouldn't even look at each other. It was a horrible feeling. I was going through hell. In less than a year I had been raped, I had found out about the sexual abuse of my sister and daughters, my husband was cheating on me, and now I wasn't speaking to my brother. My parents always taught us that family was first. With that in mind, and because I so terribly missed my brother's hugs and kisses, I made the first move to mend our relationship. God works in mysterious ways. That experience taught us quite a bit. We haven't fought, argued, or disagreed on anything since.

As much as I was hurting during that time, I enjoyed knowing that I was steps ahead of my husband and that soon he'd be in for a big surprise. For those two months I dressed in the skimpy outfits he liked, put on makeup, and did my hair every day. I gave him foot massages when he got home and sex every night. By September I had transferred the registrations of both vehicles to my name and paid off all of our credit-card debt. Then I was prepared to let him have it. It was going to go down my way. It was going to end the way I wanted it to end.

After we started being intimate again, I felt angry and sad when we were in bed. But this was the first sign that he was falling back in love with me. The changes I was making physically combined with the extra attention I was giving him were all working. We made a trip, just the two of us, to Laughlin, Nevada, and had a beautiful time. He had no clue that the shit was about to hit the fan and splatter all over his face.

At five thirty in the morning on August 1, 1998, I handed Juan his lunch just as on every other morning. "Baby, I love you," he told me. "I'm sorry if I was mean and not affectionate toward you in the past. I don't know what was wrong with me. I love you so much and I never want to lose you. When I come home from work today, I want you to be ready to go out. We'll go to dinner and then dancing. We'll have a good time, okay?"

That was exactly what I was waiting to hear. "That's sounds great, baby. I love you with all my heart too. I'll be ready."

Tenderly, I kissed my husband good-bye, knowing it was the last time I would do so. As he jumped into my Lexus ES300 (oh, yes, he always got to drive the Lexus I had bought with my real estate earnings and left me with the Ford Explorer), I decided this would be the last time he showed off *his* car to his girlfriends at work. My heart was devastated, but my mind was strong and firm. I put on the Nike sport suit he liked to see me wear and headed out the door without my wedding band. The ring that supposedly symbolized our love, our unity, our faithfulness to each other. So much for that.

My friend Cynthia was waiting outside in her truck. Juan would be furious to know that she was one of my accomplices, since he hated her guts with a passion. She drove while I rode shotgun and our friend Nacho sat in the backseat. The drive to Torrance was horrible. I couldn't wait to see the look on his face, but I was scared of how I was going to feel when he was no longer home with me. The fear didn't stop me.

When we got to the parking-garage entrance, I told the security guards that I was there to see my brother and I would be out shortly. I had Cynthia park as close to the building door as possible. Since Fairchild Fasteners was technically on federal property and I would be trespassing, I needed to be able to enter and exit quickly.

I pushed the door open, making a loud noise, which got the attention I wanted from his fellow employees. As I stomped through the warehouse, I could feel everyone's eyes on me. Some showed surprise, some showed confusion, some stared in disbelief, many seemed excited. Obviously, everyone knew what had been going on behind my back, and they knew exactly why I was there. I asked one of the employees where Juan was, and he pointed to an office door. Then I heard another coworker screaming at me, "You're not supposed to be here!"

"No duh, *menso*! Tell me something I don't know," I said as I headed toward the door and pushed it open. Juan was sitting there with another employee. When he saw me, he looked as though he had been hit over the head with an iron pole.

"Where's Maria's husband?" I asked.

His face turned different colors—first pale, then red, then blue, then pale again. I thought he was going to faint. His eyes, wide open, began to water. I could see his Adam's apple move as he swallowed hard. "What Maria?"

"The slut you've been fucking. The one with no ass. I noticed it in the video the private investigator took of you a few months ago."

He remained silent.

"If not Maria, the other skank will do. You know, Lilly, the married one."

"I don't know what you are talking about."

"The hell you don't. You, this idiot sitting with you, and all the rest of the people in this joint know what's been going on. You all just didn't know that I knew. You all thought it was funny and cute, huh? Let me tell you what's funny and cute. What's cute is there is no reason for you to come home. What's funny is that all your shit will be burning in the front yard. There will be nothing but ashes for you to pick up. Oh, and by the way, you're going to need a ride after work."

I turned around and headed back toward the doorway. Cynthia was waiting for me in the getaway car, while Nacho had already taken off in the Lexus. I had made an extra copy of the car key during the two-month "waiting period." The drive back to Compton was quiet. I couldn't believe I had gone through with it. I loved Juan so much, but I wasn't about to let my guard down now. The pain of knowing that he had slept with someone else was too much for me to handle.

The job wasn't finished yet. I had just seen *Waiting to Exhale* and I loved the scene where Angela Bassett lit all of her man's clothes on fire and then smoked a cigarette as she watched them burn. You know what happened next.

I called my family and told them to come over and look through Juan's closet and pick out anything that they wanted to take. Chiquis and I gathered the rest of his clothes and threw them in two trash cans. In went his underwear and T-shirts, his favorite Air Jordan sports outfits and shoes, his church dress suits. Juan knew how to dress, and he had a lot of nice, expensive clothes. I didn't care. I went crazy showering his belongings with the lighter fluid. I enjoyed the feeling of vengeance and accomplishment when I threw a match in each garbage can. Then I lit a cigarette (though I didn't smoke) and watched the flames as I did my best Angela Bassett impression.

Juan, who got a ride from a coworker, arrived just in time to save a few hundred dollars from the pocket of one of the burning jackets in the melting plastic trash cans. I admit it was an evil thing to do, and I regret having done it while my children were watching. I can't imagine what it must have felt like for them to see their mother hurting, but also to know that they would now be missing their stepfather in their lives, less than a year after their biological father had become a fugitive from the law.

The days after the separation were devastating. Juan moved back to his mother's home in Huntington Park, and I stayed at the home in Compton before moving to my parents' home in North Long Beach temporarily. I was not doing well financially, since I couldn't bring myself to concentrate on work. All I could think about was my on-and-off feelings for Juan. It didn't help that he would call me almost daily to try to convince me to give our relationship another try. Like all men caught red-handed, at first he was defensive. He told me I was evil and that he couldn't believe I had gone so far as to hire a private investigator to follow him around. He also couldn't believe that I had kept quiet for so many months, knowing he had cheated and focusing on making him fall in love with me again.

After I threw him out of the house and burned his clothing that August, I didn't see him again until November. We barely even spoke. He would insist that he wanted me back and that I was the only person he wanted to be with. He was remorseful about what he had done, but I still didn't want him back.

Soon after the incident Juan became depressed and kept on saying that he would do anything to show how sorry he was to have let our love down. Sometimes he would call or meet with me and demand to know when we would finally be able to put the whole dramatic nightmare behind us. He constantly begged me to forgive him and move forward with our relationship in the interest of our daughter and my three older kids. Although I sincerely wanted my children to experience stability at home and have a father figure, I didn't know if I could handle living with him knowing that he had been unfaithful. It was extremely painful to think about, and I knew it would be difficult for me to trust him again.

Every time I spoke to Juan he'd ask, "Are we getting back together? Are we going to work this out?" My answer was always no. The holidays came and it was hard to be alone with the kids and without a partner. My baby girl, Jenicka, was so little, and I started to feel guilty. Maybe I should give him another chance? I always wanted to make my relationships work, and if people sincerely apologize for their mistakes, I eventually forgive. Friends and family have often told me that this is my greatest strength, but also my greatest weakness.

In February of 1999 Juan and I got back together. He moved back into the house on Valentine's Day of that year. I told myself that if we could get through this, we could get through anything.

10

Where Are My Malandrinas At?

Nos dicen las malandrinas
porque hacemos mucho ruido
porque tomamos cerveza
y nos gusta el mejor vino.

(They call us the bad girls
Because we make a lot of noise
Because we drink beer
And we like the best wine.)

—from "Las Malandrinas"

In 1998 I recorded my *Reina de Reinas* (Queen of Queens) *corrido* album and my *Si Quieres Verme Llorar* (If You Want to See Me Cry) album at the same time. Both albums were completed during the tribulation and heartache of having found out Juan was cheating on me. In this terrible, painful period, in many ways recording these albums was strengthening. I can admit to myself that my vocals on

91

these two productions were not the best. My voice had not yet developed to its fullest potential. However, that I could even manage to record during those difficult times was like training for me. I had always finished what I began, and these projects were not going to be exceptions. This is where I learned to get things done in my career despite what I might be going through in my personal life. Little did I know that I was going to be needing this experience and strength in many other circumstances in the years to come.

In 1999, my father licensed both albums to Sony Discos, the regional Mexican division of Sony Records. They were both released that year. I was excited that my music would be distributed under a bigger label. Especially after Balboa Records did not invest in promoting my album *La Maestra* when I recorded it for them. It was a new beginning, I thought. It felt good to know that Ruben Espinoza, José Rosario, and other executives at the label actually believed in me, at least a little. Ruben wanted us to focus on the *corrido* album, since no other female at the time was recording *corridos*. It was the best way to break in, according to him and my father. José Rosario, however, thought differently. He said that I could become a great "*balada* and bolero artist." Whatever the outcome, it didn't matter much to me. What mattered was that someone, anyone, was willing to listen to and promote my music.

Unfortunately, it didn't last long. The label had become saturated with many new artists, including several of my brothers, Las Voces del Rancho, and many of the singers my dad was producing. I started to realize that it wasn't going to be beneficial for me to remain with Sony. They had many priorities, and sadly, I wasn't one of them. They simply didn't have the time for me. It was comforting to know that at least it was my brothers and my father's artists who had priority over me. I'd much rather it be them getting the attention and the promotional budget than artists who had nothing to do with our family and our record label.

At that time I recorded the CD entitled *Que Me Entierren con la Banda*, my first full *banda* (Mexican brass-band music) CD in a few years. On this album I included a *corrido* I had written entitled "Las Malandrinas." I believed in the album and especially that song, but I was worried that it wouldn't get the backing it deserved at Sony.

Around that time I met a girl who worked at Fonovisa Records. Somehow she made it to the studio when I was recording the album at Pacific Coast Recording in Long Beach. We became friends, and after she listened to a few of the songs I had included on the album, she said I should approach Fonovisa with it. I spoke to my dad about it, and he was adamant that I stay with Sony. He said they could do a better job and they supported me. I disagreed.

"Daddy, please take it to Fonovisa instead," I pleaded with him. "I believe in this album. There are a lot of good songs on it. It would make me very sad if it fell through the cracks at Sony due to lack of interest. Please, Dad. If nothing happens at Fonovisa, I would want it to be my mistake, not yours."

My mind was made up. My father knew me well enough to understand that I wasn't going to budge. He called Fonovisa and tried to get an appointment with Gilberto Moreno, then president of the label. By the time he was able to see us, I had already delivered a master copy of my "Las Malandrinas" track to various stations in Southern and Central California. I didn't have a promoter or a label to cover the expenses and knock on doors for me, so my husband drove us. I directed him to whatever stations I remembered from my first self-promotional tour in 1996 when I was delivering master copies of "La Chacalosa," which the stations never played.

Before heading out on the 5 freeway toward the 99 to Central California, we stopped by La Ley 97.9 FM. Guillermo Prince, the programmer at the station, said he liked the *corrido* and promised that I would hear it on the air before I got to the Grapevine (a windy section of the 5 freeway). To this day, his words and his kindness have remained dear to my heart. Though much of the music industry can be dirty and ugly, there will always be good-hearted people like Guillermo Prince, Pepe Garza, and others who will give you a chance and offer you their support.

Juan and I continued on my self-promotional tour for a few days. When I came back to LA, my father and I visited Mr. Moreno at Fonovisa. I was excited. This was the label that had made Carmen Jara big during the nineties. All the big-timers were at this label, including Los Tigres del Norte, Banda el Recodo, Conjunto Primavera, and Los Temerarious, among others. Maybe this would be my big chance, I thought. Without Mr. Moreno's even listening to my music, we were told that my father wouldn't get any money for its production. He wouldn't even get reimbursed for the costs he had already incurred. But we were welcome to drop off the album if we wanted. No money, no promise for promotion, no nothing.

Damn. I felt terrible. They were basically telling us that my father's production effort was not worth a dime. I was more devastated for my father than for me. I wasn't just another of his artists, I was his queen, the girl he had believed in since she was a child. I could only imagine what it felt like to hear, in front of his daughter, that what was a masterpiece production to him was a piece of shit to someone else.

After talking it through for a long time, we decided to proceed with Fonovisa. We signed a contract with the label, promising to license three productions to them, including the one with "Las Malandrinas" on it. We were reminded that my dad wouldn't be reimbursed for production costs and there were to be no marketing plans for any of my CDs. Basically all they would do was distribute it. Hopefully, I thought, they would sell at least a few CDs due to the radio airplay I had got on my own. Wherever "Las Malandrinas" was played, it was well received, which gave me a bit of self-satisfaction because it was the result of my hard work, my lyrics, my ideas, and my very own promotion. It became an underground hit in Southern California and several other areas.

I had become content with being the underdog. I enjoyed proving my disbelievers wrong. I wondered if what I was going through was normal. Every time I took a step forward, I felt as if I were knocked back. Was it this rocky for everyone? Male and female artists alike? I didn't know. I just knew that nothing came easy for me.

In 2001 my brother Lupe had his huge hit song, "Dedicatoria," which went to number one on the *Billboard* charts for both Top Latin Albums and Regional/Mexican Albums. At the time I was starting to become nationally known, but I wasn't selling out huge venues, and the little radio airplay I was getting started to disappear. A lot of people thought that I would benefit from my brother's having the number one hit on the radio, but it was quite the opposite. As soon as Lupe became really big, it became even harder for me. They stopped playing "Las Malandrinas" because they didn't want to play both my song and my brother's. When I would visit or call the stations, they would tell me, "This isn't the Rivera station." A lot of people swore that it was Lupe's fault, but I knew it wasn't. He had no control. It makes sense. You don't want to put on a radio station and hear all the Jackson 5.

I kept reminding myself that one of my idols, Chalino Sánchez, never got played on the radio before he died, but while he was living, we all knew he was the best we had. It comforted me to know that my songs became underground hits, but it was frustrating that none of the stations would play me. I would get pissed off and angry at the whole music industry. I would say, "Fuck them then, I can do it on my own. One day they will ask for me." However, I couldn't deny that getting airplay is huge, especially in LA.

Around this time the popular LA DJ Pepe Garza decided that because they wouldn't give regional Mexican music a specific category at the big award shows, he would create his own show. In 2001 he started the Premios Que Buena (later to be renamed Premios de la Radio). It was the first award show created by a regional-Mexican radio station. Lupillo was was set to perform the night of the awards ceremony, so I said to Pepe, "Let me sing my song too. Give me a chance."

Pepe listened to "Las Malandrinas" and said, "Look, it definitely has potential, but I can't have you sing the song because you are not known yet. What if I let you hand out an award?" I agreed to be a presenter and figured out a way to use the moment to my advantage.

That night when I got up to the podium, I called out, "Where are all my *malandrinas* at?" The girls went crazy and started singing my song back to me. Obviously, I knew what I was doing. I was showing Pepe that just because I wasn't a hit on LA radio, it didn't mean I wasn't known. I had to show him, not tell him. After that he started playing "Las Malandrinas" on Que Buena 105.5, one of the biggest Spanish-language stations in LA.

The first time I heard my song on the radio I was driving some clients to see a house in Compton. We were listening to Que Buena, and when my voice came through the speakers, I went crazy. "That's me!" I told them. "I'm on the radio!" They must have thought I was insane, but I didn't care. I was screaming so loudly and so happily. That's when it started. I started to get airplay outside of LA too, and that was huge for me. That said, it wasn't as if I were an overnight sensation after that. I was still clawing my way up.

Because my popularity began to grow, slowly but surely, I was able to devote myself to my singing career full-time and drop my jobs as a real estate agent and a part-time employee at Cintas Acuario Music and Cintas Acuario Publishing. As I began to get more gigs on the weekends, we decided that Juan would quit his job at Fairchild Fasteners to accompany me on the road. I finally felt better knowing that he was no longer among the women at work. It was embarrassing to me that they knew I had given him another chance. Plus, since I didn't trust him, I was always nagging him and that would cause continuous problems between us.

Despite Juan's infidelity, I must say that he was always a firm believer in my talent. He knew that I would someday be someone important in my musical genre and in the Latin community. Because I loved him and because he was so supportive, I put the cheating behind us and moved on with him by my side. I wanted the people in the industry to know that he was my husband. He served as my business manager and did all of my bookings. He also shielded me from some of the dirty aspects of the industry. I learned a lot of valuable lessons when I worked at the record label with my dad, and one of them was that sleeping your way to the top is not a myth. It happens. But it wasn't going to happen that way for me. I wanted it to be known that I was a married woman who was successful based on her talent. I never hid that I was married, and I would respect my husband to the fullest among people and artists in the industry.

Just when "Las Malandrinas" was starting to get a lot of airplay on La Ley 97.9 and Que Buena 105.5, I became pregnant with my fifth child, my second child with Juan. I was quite selfish at the time and was devastated. My music was finally being heard throughout California, Arizona, Washington, Oregon, Colorado, Illinois, and in other states. Everyone told me that having a baby would ruin my career and all that I had fought for in the past five years.

"I'm not ready to have this child now," I told Juan.

"I agree."

"I want to have an abortion."

"Fine."

That was the extent of our conversation, and then I made my appointment. But then the strangest thing happened. When I went to the clinic to have the procedure, I took the urine test confirming that I was pregnant, and then when the doctor was to suction the baby out, the fetus was nowhere to be found. The doctor said if the baby was not in my uterus, he was in my fallopian tubes, which is dangerous and possibly fatal. They took me to the hospital to monitor me. I had to lie in the hospital bed and wait to see if the fetus would come back into the uterus so they could do the procedure. I had to stay in bed because if anything burst inside me, it could kill me. I was there for a few days and still the baby was nowhere to be found. I told the doctor and nurses that I had to get out of there because I had performances in Indio that weekend. They tried to convince me not to go, but I wouldn't hear a word of it. They told me I was leaving at my own risk, and I had to sign papers to release myself so they wouldn't be held responsible. They instructed me to go to the nearest emergency room if anything happened.

I performed that Friday, Saturday, and Sunday. On Monday I came back to LA and went to the hospital to get checked again. And there the baby was, right where he was supposed to be. It was the weirdest phenomenon. I had never been one to even think about having an abortion, but this time I had, and now look at what had happened. I started to feel guilty about my decision not to have him. My baby wanted to live. I changed my mind right then and there. My little fighter would be born after all.

I continued to perform throughout the pregnancy, and the fans became so excited for me. The baby brought *la torta* (good omen). The pregnancy turned out to be the best thing that could have happened to me. I love all my children, but this little boy brought so much happiness to my life.

Johnny Angel López was born on February 11, 2001. The following day, February 12, Que Buena started playing "Querida Socia." Many other stations followed its example, and in weeks I had a second hit on the radio. The original singer of the song, Diana Reyes, was getting major airplay on stations in Mexico. Her label was rumored to be bringing her on a promotional tour with her version of "Querida Socia." Their plan was to take the territory that I had conquered with my version.

For that reason, Fonovisa contacted me and told me to get ready for my first promo tour with the label. I doubt that they cared much about the success of the song; it mattered more to them that a competing record label would even attempt to conquer their territory. Regardless, this was how the label started to promote me, and this was the song that brought me national and international attention.

11

Lupillo Rivera's Sister

Pienso que es preferible sufrir a solas
Mi cruel tormento.

(*I think it's better to suffer on my own*
My cruel torment.)
—from "Sufriendo a Solas"

In 2001 I went to Miami to promote my new album. I was still unknown in that market, so all of the announcers insisted on introducing me as "Jenni Rivera, Lupillo Rivera's sister." It started to get under my skin. I was proud of my brother, of course, but I was also determined that one day they would introduce me as just "Jenni Rivera."

I was most excited to go on Don Francisco's *Sábado Gigante* on Univision, one of my favorite shows. In June 2001, when I first sat down with him, Don Francisco showed a welcoming video of my parents, brothers, sister, and kids. When the part about my kids came on, I began to cry. I knew I was being seen all over the world and that my mascara was probably going to start dripping down my face, so I tried to hold it back. But I couldn't hide my emotions. All my life I've worked so hard to give my five babies everything I never had, and that was a wonderful moment of realization for me. I was making good on my promise. I was making my kids proud. One day they would be able to look back and say, "My mother gave everything she had to give us a better life." There has never been anything more important to me than that.

I wiped away my tears as Don Francisco and I started the interview. One of the first questions he asked was "Who is older, Lupillo or you?" I had loved him before, but now I loved him so much more.

"I am two years older than Lupillo," I told him. "I am thirty-two, but I look twenty-two."

He started to laugh, and the audience laughed with him. We had chemistry right off the bat, and still do to this day. As an interviewer he makes you feel safe, and I talked to him about times in my life that I had never revealed to anyone else. I briefly told him about the rape that had occurred in 1997 (that was the only time I ever publically discussed what happened that night). I told him of how I used to work at the swap meets or collect scrap metal for change, and how I was now working as a secretary at my parents' record label.

Before our interview was over, he asked me to stay and cohost the show with him for the following three hours. I was so honored and so grateful. *Sábado Gigante* is one of the most entertaining shows in the US Latin market and has been for many years. Getting the chance to sit with Don Francisco gave me the exposure I needed with Latinos from different cultures, not just my already-established Mexican following. Outside of Southern California I was a nobody. Don Francisco changed that. After that interview aired I got letters from Guatemalans, Salvadoreans, Cubans, Nicaraguans, Dominicans, and Puerto Ricans. In the following years I became one of the most frequent guests on *Don Francisco Presenta,* where I was invited to perform, and that has always meant a lot to me. Don Francisco is a wonderful man, and every time I've sat down with him I've had such a good time. When he spoke to me off air, he told me how much he respected my hard work and determination. He also told me that I was "Two R's: Real and Ratings!"

Though I still had a long way to go on the national and international stage, I had become a local celebrity in the Hispanic parts of LA such as Long Beach, Huntington Park, and South Gate. Fans started to gather outside my home on Keene Avenue in Compton. They would show up in the middle of the night asking for pictures and autographs. Oftentimes they would be drunk, yelling my name, or knocking on the front door. Don't get me wrong, I was flattered, and a part of me couldn't believe people were actually that interested in me. But another part of me wanted peace and quiet, and I worried that it might not be safe for my children.

Though I had quit my job at the real estate office earlier that year, I still loved to search around Southern California for properties. I saw a listing for a gorgeous house in Corona, a city forty miles east of LA. I got in the car and drove to see it in person. When I got off the 91 freeway and drove the four miles leading up to the driveway, I passed horse and dairy farms. We weren't in Compton anymore. As soon as I pulled up to the house, I fell in love with it. The seven-bedroom, six-bath, seven-thousand-square-foot ranch was set on an acre of wide-open land. And the price was just too good to pass up.

I moved into the house in July of 2001 with Juan and my five children. As we unpacked, I said to Chiquis, "Remember when we lived in the cold garage in Long Beach and I used to ride you on the back of my bike to day care at six in the morning? I used to promise you that one day I was going to get us a big house like this."

"I remember," she said. "And I knew you would do it too."

It was an amazing moment for me, yet in the back of my mind I was wondering what I was doing with my husband, who was not really bringing anything to the table. I knew Juan loved me and I knew I loved him, but that simply wasn't enough. It didn't guarantee happiness. We had been together for six years and I still can't really pinpoint the reason why we weren't able to get along. Was it that I had become too determined to make it as an artist? Did I become buried in reaching my goal? Did he resent that I was becoming more popular? Was he scared of losing me to the greatly demanding record industry and all that came along with it? Or was it that I never got over that he had cheated on me during the most difficult time in my life?

Deep inside, as much as I loved him, I have to admit that I did still resent him for having deceived me after I had done so much for him. I didn't trust him anymore, and that caused serious marital problems between us. If I acted as if everything were okay, that was also a problem. He'd say that because I was now JENNI RIVERA, I thought I was better than him, which was ironic, since I was still trying to get the rest of the world to call me JENNI RIVERA.

One night Juan and I got into a big fight, and I called Rosie, Gladyz, and two more friends who were all going through heartbreak at the time. We went to a hole-in-the-wall bar where I knew they had a good Mexican band playing. As soon as we sat down, Rosie told us, "There is no crying tonight. The first person who cries has to put their underwear in the middle of the table."

By the end of the night five pairs of thongs were in the center of the table, and we were all too drunk to drive home, so we called Lupillo to come pick us up.

When he got there, he said, "Why the fuck are your thongs on the table?"

"Pupi," I said, "will you sing for us?"

"No, Jenni. I'm here to pick you up and go. Let's go."

"Please. I want to hear 'Sufriendo a Solas.' "

Lupillo couldn't say no to me. Especially when I was drunk and heartbroken.

He got up onstage and the crowd couldn't believe it was him. As soon as he was finished singing the song, people shouted out requests and cheered for more as they handed him tequila shots. In true Rivera style he couldn't say no to his fans. And in true Rivera style he "accidentally" got buzzed onstage. I joined him onstage and we sang a full free concert for the patrons of the dive bar, as my underwear sat on a table in the back.

In September I had a radio interview in New York. I was on another of my diets and got stupid drunk on three martinis. I was still going through a lot with Juan, and I was just pissed at the world. We were in a taxi riding uptown when I rolled down the window and screamed *Fuck you*s into the night. "Fuck you, Juan. And fuck you, Trino. Fuck you, streetlamps. Fuck you, New York. And fuck you, trash bags on the sidewalk!" This was just after 9/11, and the whole city was on edge and eerily quiet. And there I was, this crazy Mexican chick, screaming "Fuck you" to the world.

The taxi driver couldn't get rid of Rosie and me fast enough once we got to our hotel. We were staying in this huge, fancy place that the radio station was paying for. It was ridiculously expensive, and I would never have picked it. If I had been paying, we'd have been staying at a Best Western or whatever was the cheapest hotel in New York. But instead we strolled our drunk asses into this fancy-ass lobby. This very proper Asian lady was walking down the sweeping staircase in a red coat that probably cost enough money to feed a small country. "Fuck you, lady in the red coat!" I screamed at her. She didn't know what to do, and she definitely didn't know who I was. She paused for a second, then turned and went running back up the stairs.

"Sister!" Rosie yelled at me. "What did she do to you?"

"I didn't like her red coat. It was ugly. And you know what? Fuck your mother."

"Well, fuck your father."

"Fuck your brothers."

Rosie took a deep breath and said, "Fuck your fucking fans."

She knew that was crossing the line. "Now you've gone too far!" I yelled at her. "Leave my fans alone! I don't want to play anymore."

My family and friends all knew that they could talk mess and joke around about my mama, my daddy, my brothers. I could take it. But not my fans.

When I returned home from that trip, I walked into my new home and was greeted with my first big stack of fan mail. It was as if they had heard me defending them in the lobby of that ridiculous rich person's hotel. That night I opened the envelopes one by one. People wrote such beautiful words of support and inspiration. They talked about how much they appreciated my music for giving women a strong voice, about how my lyrics helped them through difficult times. They said they had seen me on *Don Francisco Presenta* talking about such personal issues and it made them feel as if they were not alone. What these fans never knew is that they made me feel as if I were never alone either.

That year I hired an assistant to help me with the mail because I wanted to correspond directly with everyone who took the time to write to me. I also hired someone to travel with me and carry a Polaroid camera so when people came up to me, they could have a photo on the spot. I had these people on my staff before I even had a steady manager.

My fans were so special to me because they loved me even though they didn't have to, and that always touched me so deeply. They were not related to me. They didn't have to stand by me when I made mistakes or took risks that everyone else thought I shouldn't take. They didn't have to have my back when I got in public feuds or if somebody talked mess about me. They didn't have to believe and support me before I was anything.

Yet, from the very beginning, they did.

12

Busting Out

Se las voy a dar a otro,
porque tú no las mereces.

(*I'll give my love to another*
because you do not deserve it.)
                    —from "Se las Voy a Dar a Otro"

People often ask about the moment I knew I had "made it."
I don't know about other artists, but for me there was never a single
day or event that I could point to and say, "That was it." It wasn't the
first time I heard myself on the radio, or that stack of fan mail, or the
first time I was recognized on the street. It was a series of events, a
collection of small and big moments that built up to make me believe
that maybe, just maybe, I had staying power.

In November of 2001 I went to Vicente Fernández's concert at the
Gibson Amphitheatre (which was then called the Universal Amphitheatre). My whole family looks up to Vicente Fernández, and every
year we all went to at least one of his concerts. The first time I saw
him perform was at the Million Dollar Theater in downtown LA dur-

ing the 1970s. I was about four or five years old, and my dad and I went to take Polaroids to sell to the crowd. At one point during the concert Vicente saw me and asked me to get onstage for a picture with him. I was so proud. Nobody is bigger in Mexican music than Vicente. I grew up listening to his music and idolizing him. He was huge back in the seventies, and more than two decades later he was still going strong and singing to sold-out Gibson crowds for three nights in a row.

As we walked to our seats that night in 2001, people started to cheer and go nuts. Naturally I thought it was for Vicente. It took me a minute to figure out that they were all looking at me, calling my name, and asking for a picture or autograph. Vicente saw the commotion, and once again he invited me onstage with him, but this time he wanted me to sing. I was so nervous, but kept telling myself to be cool and not to show it. I sang "Por un Amor" as he watched from the stage. I will never forget the words he spoke to the crowd when we were done with the song: "*Esta mujer no le pide nada a cualquier artista de aqui o alla,*" meaning that this woman does not lack anything that any female artist from here or there (the United States and Mexico) has. I was flying high that night and for many nights to come.

Less than a year later, in 2002, I was nominated for a Latin Grammy for Best Banda Album for *Se las Voy a Dar a Otro* (I'll Give It to Another). When I got the news, my mind immediately flashed back to that desperate night at the Compton house when I was watching the 1998 Grammy show with my children, holding baby Jenicka in my arms, wondering if my husband was cheating on me, and hearing my Chiquis and Jacqie tell me that I could one day be nominated for a Grammy. Four years later my daughters' words were coming true.

The show was on September 18, 2002. I was fighting with Juan, as usual, so I decided that I wanted my parents, my brothers, and my sister to come with me instead. We all met at my parents' house. Everyone was running late, of course. This was our family's first big awards show, and if there was one thing that was perfectly clear to me, it was that I never wanted to live through an amazing moment on my own. I always wanted my family to be around me to share in it. Even if it did take forever to get all eight Riveras out the door.

My four brothers drove me to the event in a convertible, and I sat on the top of the car as if I were in the hood and I was the queen of the parade, just as I had all those years ago for my quinceañera. We walked down the carpet together and then into the Kodak Theatre. It was all so surreal.

Mom, Rosie, and my brothers sat up in the balcony, and my dad sat next to me on the lower level with all the other nominees. When my name was announced, the cheering and applause did not stop. It gave me the chills. As the applause continued, I looked at my dad with tears in my eyes. He was crying too. It was as though all of the heartbreak, the hardships, the hard work, had led us to this one moment, in the middle of the Kodak Theatre in Hollywood. I didn't win—Banda Cuisillos did—but to me that didn't matter. I was just happy to be there. I know everyone says that and it sounds like bullshit, but I swear it's true. I felt as if I won by being the public's favorite. They didn't clap or cheer like that for anybody else. That one event gave me so much more confidence that my career was moving in the right direction.

Of course, I was still making mistakes and stumbling along the way. For example, that year I became friends with a female disc jockey named Rocío Sandoval, who went by the nickname La Peligrosa. We had a good time during and after my interview with her, and I felt that

I could trust her. I let her into my life and told her very private things. I thought that she respected me, that she respected our friendship, but that was clearly not the case. The next time I went on her radio show, she took a lot of cheap shots at me by asking questions directly related to secrets I had shared with her. I couldn't believe she was going there. She also acted surprised that I had five children, as if she didn't already know, and she made it sound as if it were something for me to be ashamed of. I have always been so proud to be a mother, and she knew that. She also knew that a lot of my fan base was made up of single mothers who related to me, so I didn't think it was too smart on her part to have brought it up in such a negative way.

I could forgive all of this, but the day after the Que Buena Awards she took it too far. She bad-mouthed my mother and my family and that sent me over the edge. My mother is a kind, respectable lady, and La Peligrosa said my mother was expecting red-carpet treatment at events simply because she was "the mother of the Riveras." To this day I do not know what pushed her to make those comments; I only know that she was way off base. My mother has never expected red-carpet treatment in her life. Anyone who has ever met her knows I'm not lying. Shortly after, Isis Sauceda, a reporter at the LA Spanish-language newspaper *La Opinión,* published an interview with La Peligrosa where she was quoted as saying, "The Riveras are very un-grateful people." I don't know who she was referring to, but it didn't matter, I was officially offended and pissed.

A few weeks later that same reporter, Isis Sauceda, interviewed me and asked me about La Peligrosa's comments. I responded that I had nothing to say and that I wasn't angry at all, but I simply felt sorry for her and hoped that God would cure her of that horrible disease called jealousy. I said I hoped her bad feelings toward me would dis-appear and that her heart would heal.

The reaction to my comments was intense. The media wanted

to know more about who said what. I guess La Peligrosa thought I would keep quiet about her problems since she was a prominent disc jockey at the radio station that had opened the doors for me. But my dignity was on the line. My self-respect as a daughter, mother, sister, and woman would have been shattered if I had let her talk about me and my family without defending myself. It got out of hand, and one day one of the heads of Que Buena asked me to refrain from commenting on the situation anymore because it was hurting the image of his radio station. I like and respect this man very much, so I honored his request. I got together with La Peligrosa, and we both agreed not to take the matter any further.

In my career I've learned to respect the media because they can make or break you as an artist, but I refused to bow down to them if my pride or dignity was at stake. I refused to stop being myself, regardless of what it might cost me.

The drama with La Peligrosa also made me realize that if I was going to stick up for my dignity in my professional life, I had to do it in my personal life as well. So I decided to make a break with Juan once and for all.

No matter how much I tried to make it work with Juan, we couldn't get it right. The problems began to take over my entire life, to the point where I found myself bringing my emotional problems onstage with me and into media interviews and not being able to give my best to my fans.

Nothing in my life felt complete. I wasn't yet where I wanted to be in my music career, but I couldn't focus on actually getting there because my relationship was growing more and more dramatic. I realized that if I stayed in my marriage, I would never make it as an artist. So I had to make a decision: either I had to stay in the troubled relationship that was continuously bringing problems to my career, and live with the consequences, or I had to let the relationship go and focus on my career and on getting ahead in life. I didn't know what to do.

In late June 2002, Juan made a mistake that helped me make that difficult decision. One night, after one of our famous fights, I walked into our bedroom while Juan was in the shower. I wanted to talk to him and hopefully resolve the quarrel we'd had earlier that evening. As I made my way toward the bathroom to surprise him, I was in for a surprise myself. I saw his cell phone sitting on the nightstand on the side of his bed. For some strange reason I picked it up and began running through his call log. I noticed that the last call he had made was less than thirty minutes earlier. It was to a 562 area code. The *67 that registered before the number jumped out at me. He had obviously called someone and didn't want to have his number come up on the person's caller ID.

Of course I pressed redial on his phone. And of course a woman answered.

I hung up and walked to the bathroom where he was sitting on the step by the Jacuzzi with a bath towel wrapped around his waist, nice and fresh after his shower. I immediately confronted him. "Who is this?" I demanded, pushing redial once again while setting his phone on speaker mode. I saw the same stupid look he'd had on his face when I'd confronted him the first time he cheated. He didn't know what to say. I went crazy. I began throwing whatever I could find at him—drinking glasses, colognes (his, of course), vases, anything I could find to hurt him.

"I didn't do anything!" he screamed. "I just called her. I just got the number!" He claimed it never went past a mere phone call, but it didn't matter anymore. In my mind, the intention was there. He had crossed a line. My heart loved him, but my mind hated him for being so stupid and putting our marriage at risk once again. I told him to stay at his mother's house in Huntington Park. I needed some time alone.

He stayed at his mother's one-bedroom home for a couple of weeks, but he was constantly begging me to let him come back. He would tell me how much he missed me and the kids, but I couldn't help but wonder if he really just missed the new lifestyle he had become accustomed to in Corona. The doubt continually ran through my mind.

Eventually, I let him come back home, but from then on the roller coaster was on a serious downhill roll, making me sick to my stomach. He was going to give me a fucking ulcer.

After all that happened, I just couldn't be the devoted and understanding wife I had vowed to be when we got married. Fights and heated discussions came and went, and every time I would be less and less fazed by them. Once he came home with a beautiful mink coat as a form of apology, which would have been a nice gesture if he'd used his own money to buy it. Whenever I wore that mink, I would walk around saying, "Don't you love the fur coat that Juan bought me with my money?"

Oftentimes when we were on the road, we would have arguments before, after, or even during my performances. He didn't care if I was going to go onstage; he would pick a fight with me right as I was walking up there, and I'd be all messed up. I wanted to give my best to my fans; after all, they had paid to see me and they didn't care if I had problems or not. To give my best I had to be in the best emotional state, and he wasn't allowing me to do that.

Sometimes he would stay in the hotels and watch TV while I went out and made the dough. On occasion our confrontations would occur in the presence of my band members and road managers. One night after I had a performance in Utah, we had a major fight. The television in the room was thrown around and my performance clothes were dumped into the pool. Everyone found out. I felt horrible. I felt embarrassed. More and more people knew the type of life I was living.

I was so angry that I left him in that hotel room in Utah. He had nothing. No transportation, no wallet, no driver's license, no money. Nothing. He pissed me off so badly that I didn't care if and how he made it home to California. I had to keep moving. I wasn't about to let the difficulties in my relationship stop me from attaining the success I was working toward. My talent was for sure. My relationship with Juan was not. I would not be held back.

On New Year's Eve 2002 I was sitting with my brother Juan at my parents' house. We were talking about what our resolutions would be for 2003.

"This year," I told my brother, "I will leave my husband for good. I will be happily divorced by the time we bring in 2004."

He looked and me and laughed. "You're crazy, Chay. What kind of resolution is that? No wonder you guys can't work it out."

I thought otherwise. I had tried long enough to make it work. I had gone through hell and back with this guy. He had cheated on me when I most needed him. I had forgiven him and had another child. I'd worked diligently on my career to achieve a better financial situation for my kids and family. How was I going to get any further in my career if I constantly had to fight the fights? But it wasn't just about my career. It was also about my kids. In my anger with Juan I would get physically violent. I broke the house phone over his head when I found out he had been having phone conversations with yet another woman. I didn't want my children to live with the constant racket of domestic violence in yet another home. And I didn't want the two young children I had with Juan to even know what it was to live that way. They didn't ask to be born. I brought them into the world and it was my responsibility that they lived happy, healthy lives. It was also up to me to give them a better life than the one we had lived before. I wanted the best for my children and I knew I wouldn't be able to offer it to them if I didn't free myself from the man who was holding me back.

A few weeks after I made my resolution, somebody told me that Juan was partying at a club while I was performing in Mexico. Nice, huh? March came along, and instead of celebrating his birthday, we opted not to even speak to each other.

April 4, 2003. I had no gigs lined up for the weekend, so Juan and I decided to go to the Banda el Recodo concert at the Gibson Amphitheatre. We had a good time with Renán Almendárez Coello (El Cucuy), members of his crew, and other staff of La Nueva 101.9. We sang and drank, and Juan and I spent some quality time together. It was the last time we would ever do so.

The following morning I planned to go shopping for something to wear to his friend Mike's wedding that night. Since Mike was a high school friend of his, I wanted to make sure Juan approved of what I wore. It always mattered to me how his friends and family members saw me. Before I left the house, I answered some e-mails and comments on my website and my forum on Univision.com. He hated it when I did that. He said I spent way too much time responding to my fans' questions. I disagreed and would do it anyway, in part to get to know my fans better and in part just to be rebellious.

When I left for the mall, he advised me to be back at 5:00 p.m., yet I didn't get back until 5:30 p.m. I rushed into the house excitedly. Juan was in the bathroom and was pissed.

"I thought I told you I wanted to leave at five p.m."

"I know, baby. I'm sorry. I couldn't find anything I liked. I will be ready in a few minutes."

"If you hadn't been wasting your time on the Internet chatting with your fans, we'd be leaving already," he snapped back.

"I said I would be ready fast, Juan. Don't make me bring up shit that you've done. We both know you're quite good at wasting time on doing things you shouldn't do."

I was beginning to get irritated. We went back and forth until he threatened to go to the wedding without me.

"I dare you," I said. Five minutes later I watched him drive off as I looked out the bathroom window. I told myself I would give him thirty minutes to call or come back home, otherwise he would regret it. He called back thirty-five minutes later. I did not pick up. Five minutes too late was the final straw.

I got dressed and went out with my friend Erika, whose birthday had been the day before. We went to celebrate at the Mirage, a nightclub in Artesia. We had a blast. It felt amazing to be free for at least one night. No Juan. No problems. No arguments. Just Erika and me, the hip-hop music, and a few shots of tequila. I was determined to be happy with or without my husband.

In my heart I knew it was over. I knew exactly what I had to do to let him know that I was serious. I spent the night at Erika's house in Anaheim. My kids were home with the nanny and I asked her to stay until Juan got home. I didn't return home until ten the following morning. I had intentionally crossed that line.

After that, we didn't speak to each other for days. Not a word. Nor did I cook or attend to his needs. No sex. No nothing. I slept in the living room and he slept in the bed, as he usually did when we had fights. He tried to make up on various occasions, and when he realized that I wasn't giving in, he tried to get to me through the kids. But I was done.

On April 23, 2003, three days after Easter, I filed for divorce and had his sister, Maria, serve him with the divorce papers. No more messing around. For two months we lived like strangers in the same house. Though I was determined to go through with the divorce, it did hurt me to know that it was all coming to a crashing end. I loved him dearly but I didn't like him anymore. The physical attraction was still there, but the mental attraction was long gone. He had hurt me too much and made too many stupid mistakes. I could not longer respect him or myself.

Juan had been managing a lot of my career, and I decided that was the first thing I had to change. I had worked on and off with a booking manager named Gabriel Vazquez and his partner, Ariel. When I knew Juan and I were headed for divorce, I asked them to do my bookings full time. Then my attorney, Anthony Lopez, introduced me to a business manager named Pete Salgado. Anthony asked Pete to "see what you can do with her," since nobody in the industry was taking me seriously and I was still considered a novelty act as Lupillo's sister.

Pete had just finished working with the popular group Los Tucanes de Tijuana and he was a lot like me: no-nonsense, focused, and determined. We immediately bonded and started talking BIG. I asked him, "Why can't I be like Mary J. Blige?" And he responded, "You can. You will." It was so far-fetched at the time, but we were two dreamers who could see the same thing.

I also had a publicist who had an in at the Ford Theatre in LA. I was intent on singing at a venue other than a nightclub, and so we used her connections to set me a date for my first true concert: Sunday, July 6, 2003. Four days after my thirty-fourth birthday.

The Ford Theatre has one thousand seats. At the time the theater didn't have access to Ticketmaster, so if fans wanted to buy tickets, they had to go to the box office in Hollywood. Shit, I thought, how the hell was I going to fill a thousand seats? No fans were going to want to make an extra trip to Hollywood just to buy tickets. We started to promote the show on blogs and on my Myspace page (we didn't have the benefit of Facebook and Twitter back then), and fans would write in and say how many tickets they wanted. Then Rosie, Gladyz, my brothers, and Pete got into their cars and drove all over Southern California to hand-deliver the tickets. I was determined to make that concert a success for many reasons, the main one being it was the first event I ever coordinated without Juan. I had to prove that I could do this on my own.

We worked to sell the tickets throughout the month of June. Chiquis, in her last year of high school, began hearing rumors that her stepdad had been seen with girls at the Hacienda, a nightclub in Norco. She would hear different stories each week about which strip club, nightclub, or leg contest he had been at on the previous weekend. She was so embarrassed that Juan would dare to act the fool at some place so close to home. Her friends, not knowing that Juan and I were getting a divorce, would tell her that her stepdad was cheating on her mom. She was devastated to know that her classmates thought her mother was being stepped out on.

Sooner than I could imagine, the rumors started spreading well beyond the high school chatter. Juan and I had agreed not to let anyone know about our divorce because we saw how Lupillo's divorce the year before had become messy and turned into a media fiasco. We didn't want to go through the same thing. But Juan was acting like a crazy man and partying hard night after night. Since he had been in my music videos, people knew who he was, especially my fans. Whenever any of my fans would see him out on the town acting like a single man, they would call and write to the radio stations. Word on the street was "Jenni Rivera is getting played on. Jenni is getting done wrong." I started to get calls from radio stations and disc jockeys telling me what my fans had reported.

Knowing that a quiet divorce wasn't going to happen, I began to feel stupid. The strong-woman image I had created for my fans and the industry was being tarnished. To maintain my dignity I had to speak up.

On June 30, 2003, I had a radio interview with Thomas Rubio, a disc jockey at Que Buena 105.5. We were supposed to talk about my upcoming concert. A few weeks earlier, he had approached me about the situation with Juan. I had told him I wasn't ready to speak about it. By now the story was much bigger and had started to get a bit out of hand. During the interview he asked me, "We've noticed that you always take your husband everywhere, but for a few months now, you haven't. What's going on?" I clarified that we had started divorce proceedings two months before, and that technically Juan was a free man. That's how my parents found out.

The following day I was invited to perform a track I had done with Akwid at their CD release party at the House of Blues. Quite a bit of media were there. As I went down the press line, none of the reporters questioned me about Juan or my interview with Thomas Rubio. But at the end of the line Magaly Ortiz, a reporter from Univision's *Primer Impacto*, did ask if I was getting a divorce. She had heard the interview. I had no choice but to confirm.

The next day, my birthday, the news went national. After the gossip had been discussed on *Primer Impacto*, all the other Spanish entertainment-news outlets picked up the story. Since it was a public record, Jessica Maldonado of *El Gordo y la Flaca* was able to get a copy of my petition for divorce from Riverside County Court. She also got her hands on the counterdivorce papers that Juan's attorney had filed. Juan had moved out almost a month earlier, on June 6, but not before asking me for $10,000 to get an apartment. All I wanted was to get away from him, so I gave him the money. With that money he hired an attorney and asked him to file a demand for spousal support.

Jessica made sure to report on it. It became a big deal in the Spanish media. In the Latin community, it's unheard of that a woman should pay a man spousal support.

My concert at the Ford was just four days after the news broke. We had sold eight hundred tickets by hand-delivering them. Hours before I was set to go onstage, the remaining two hundred tickets were all gone too. I couldn't believe it. I had sold out my first concert.

Of course my whole family was sitting front and center. I was wearing all of these beautiful Mexican mariachi dresses and I would change between sets. One of the dresses ripped in the back while I was singing, so I got through the song and then told everybody what had happened. I called my wardrobe stylist onto the stage to fix it, so out he came with a needle and thread and began sewing me up from the back as I joked around with him. "Is it my butt?" I asked him. "Be honest. Did I gain weight?" I have always believed that it is better to own the embarrassment than to hide from it. The crowd loved it. That night, I listened to a thousand people laugh with me, cheer for me, cry and sing along with me. Regardless of what was going on in my personal life, I felt that I was going to be okay.

Meanwhile, Juan was questioned wherever he went. Many people looked down on him. How could he ask for support from a single mother of five? Was he not healthy enough or man enough to support himself? My family, my kids, and I felt the same way. The divorce proceedings began and were not pretty. I vowed that I would never forgive him for taking money from my children. My brothers wanted to kick his ass. Rosie egged his car. For once I was the rational Rivera, and instead of lashing out at him, I committed myself to my music more than ever. By this time I had learned that there is no better revenge than success and happiness (though that doesn't mean I was going to stop my sister from egging his beloved truck). My career was on the rise, and though it pissed me off to have to hand over my hard-earned money to him, I was thankful that it wasn't the other way around. Instead I sang him a song, "Las Mismas Costumbres," with lyrics that told him just how I felt: "With affection I healed your wounds. And today I pay lawsuits in court."

13

La Gran Señora

Tenemos que hablar de mujer a mujer
hay que dejar unas cosas en claro.

(*We need to talk woman to woman*
we have some things to clear up.)
—from "La Gran Señora"

As I was going through my breakup with Juan, I was also dealing with my parents' forty-two-year marriage falling apart and my beautiful sister going through a deep depression, which I felt responsible for.

Rosie never dealt with her sexual abuse with intense counseling or therapy. Instead she started turning to drugs and alcohol, and for a while she became promiscuous. We would go out to clubs together and she would wear these short miniskirts. "Can that skirt get any shorter?" I'd ask her. She'd explain that it was for practical reasons: it made it easier for the pee to come out and the penis to come in. Rosie and I always joked around about sex, and we'd say to each other, "You're such a whore." The only proper response to that was "Well, you're such a slut." Coming from anyone else, those words would have started a brawl, but in our world they were terms of endearment. We both knew that it came from a place of love.

I knew her substance abuse and promiscuity were a result of the sexual abuse, and I never judged her or shamed her, but it was hard to watch my baby sister dealing with her pain in this way. In 2002 she was seeing a guy and she got pregnant. The day that she told him, he left her. For the first two or three months she would cry all day and all night. My brothers were ready to beat his ass. "That won't help her," I told them. "That's not what she wants or needs." I understood what it was like to be pregnant and on your own, just wishing that the father of your unborn child would come back to you to love you the way you needed to be loved.

I called her ex and tried to get him to come around. "We don't judge you," I assured him. "We're here to help you." But he had made up his mind. He wasn't coming back.

Then, when Rosie was about six months pregnant, Mom dropped a bomb on the family that would change us forever. In December of 2002, after we attended the Premios de la Radio awards, she asked us all to a family meeting at her house. It was almost midnight and I was sitting there with my brothers, Rosie, and my mother, waiting for Dad to come inside. He was circling the block in his car, refusing to join us. All my brothers were asking what was going on and why Dad was acting so strange. Mom finally broke down and told us: he was cheating on her.

It hit us all like a punch to the gut. "If you don't believe me, I have evidence," she said. "I hired a private investigator and there is video." She said she had learned to do that from me. Though I was so sad, I was also proud of her for deciding she wasn't going to take it any-more. We all told her we didn't need to see any video, we believed her. One of us asked Mom, "Could you ever forgive him?"

That's when she told us the secret she had been keeping from us our whole lives. Dad had always cheated on her, from the time she was first pregnant at fifteen years old. It was the reason she was always afraid of getting pregnant. That's when he would step out the most. It was also the reason she didn't have any friends. Every time she brought another woman around, my dad would flirt with her and often end up sleeping with her. It was so hard to hear her tell us this. It was so hard to know that she had been keeping this inside for forty-two years. But the most difficult part to hear was how my mother had warned my father long ago that if he was going to sleep around, he should at least be careful not to get anyone else pregnant. That would absolutely crush her. But now he had done just that.

Finally Dad came inside. Someone asked him if it was true, and he just sat there in silence. Juan begged my dad, crying, "Please fix this family. This is all I have. Say you're sorry. This is going to tear us apart."

We were all grown adults with kids and lives of our own, yet at that moment we were all children again, desperate to save our parents from divorce. The meeting ended without an admission or an apology from Dad. We all left, heartbroken for our mother and feeling helpless that we could ever change anything. Rosie didn't leave, though. She was living there and already dealing with how the father of her unborn child had just left her. Now she was stuck in a home where the tension was so thick you could barely breathe.

For the next few months my parents lived under the same roof, but did not say a word to each other. Dad wouldn't move out because he said he had worked his whole life to pay for that home. Mom wouldn't move out because she was afraid that my father's mistress and his new child would move in. Meanwhile, we were all watching to see what would happen. This was the first time in forty-two years of marriage that Mom had ever spoken against my father. The first time she refused to cook or clean for him, the first time she kicked him out of their bedroom and made him sleep on his office floor, the first time she refused to turn a blind eye. We watched their relationship crumble before our eyes and couldn't do anything to stop it.

"I want him to apologize," Mom said to us, "I want him to respect me. I want him to love me. You guys don't understand what it means to go through your whole life not feeling loved. Not being respected." But I knew. I had been through it with Trino and then Juan. I assured her that I would stand by her no matter what she decided to do.

Mom was not forgiving him, but she was hoping that he would stop seeing the other woman so they could fix their issues. Yet Mom would find out from friends or neighbors that he was still with the mistress. We found out that the mistress was married to one of my dad's business associates. We knew her. She'd come over to our house multiple times. She had first tried to get with one of my brothers. She went down the list until she finally snagged my dad, and we all felt that she was just after the money.

Dad was sleeping on the floor in his office, which upset some of my brothers. "Well, he can get a bed," I told them. "It's his own damn fault." Onstage I would cry for my parents, but I never told the fans what was going on. My parents were still living together, and I think we were all hoping they would work it out, but I knew better. Because I could do little else but stand by my mother's side, I wrote a song called "La Gran Señora." It is about a woman addressing her man's mistress and telling her, "What's mine is mine. I won't let go. I will defend my honor. I am his lady." The media all thought it was about me. I never corrected them because I didn't want my parents' issues to become public. When I started writing songs, I wrote about party girls and drinking and fictional drug lords. As I grew as an artist, the songs became a way for me to work through my personal issues and send a message. No matter how old you are, watching your parents suffer is so painful. "La Gran Señora" helped me to process that pain.

Mom and Dad started speaking, minimally, when Rosie had her baby girl Kassandra in March of 2003. Kassey became the light in that house. Everyone could gather around her, and if my parents had any communication in that first year, it was all about Kassey.

Rosie gained eighty pounds during her pregnancy, and after she had the baby, she gained even more. She was depressed and stuck. I couldn't stand to see her that way, and I felt totally responsible. I knew that a lot of her depression stemmed from the sexual abuse, and I had to figure out a way to help her. One afternoon I walked into my parents' house and saw her sitting on the couch, crying.

"What's wrong, Samalia?" I asked her. Samalia is one of the many nicknames I have for Rosie.

"I'm so fat. I can't lose this weight. My baby's father is never going to come back to me if I stay like this."

Inside my heart was breaking, but I knew that babying her was not going to solve anything. Plus, it has never been my style. "Well, you have a choice," I told her. "You can either sit here and be a fatass for the rest of your life, or you can get up and do something about it. Tell me what you want. Tell me out loud."

"I want to be skinny."

"Why?"

"Because I want to buy normal clothes. I want to feel beautiful."

"You have to envision it and work at it. I'll help you, but you have to make this choice. I want to know today, are you going to do it?"

"Yes."

Then I said the line I became so well known for in my circle: "We'll go to TJ if you want." We had always gone to Tijuana when we were sick because we never had any medical insurance. It is also the place people go when they want to be nipped, tucked, and sucked. "We'll get you liposuction," I told her. "Do you want that?" I figured if she wasn't going to go to a proper therapist, a plastic surgeon would work just as well. Maybe better.

"I want a gastric bypass," she said.

"What is that?"

"I have been researching. It is when they make your stomach smaller. It works better long term."

I asked around among industry friends and they led me to Dr. Buenrostro. That June we went to TJ and Rosie had her surgery. She started to lose weight right away. I was so excited for her and thought this would get her out of her depression, but she still seemed down.

For the next three months Rosie descended into an even deeper depression due to the shame of the sexual abuse and the rejection of the man she loved. She stopped wearing makeup, she only dressed in sweats, she rarely showered. It was so painful to see her beautiful spirit slipping away. Again I felt this was my fault. Ever since Rosie had been a baby, I'd vowed to be her protector and to make sure she was happy. When I found out about the sexual abuse, I broke down, knowing that I had failed her and my daughters. From that day forward I made a promise to them and to myself that I would spend the rest of my life making things right. But I was still failing Rosie. I didn't know what to do.

At the same time, my parents, who never spoke a bad word about each other for forty-two years, were now calling me to complain about each other. In between those phone calls I got a message from my lawyer. My soon-to-be-ex-husband was claiming that he had contributed to developing my career as an artist and therefore deserved to be paid for it. According to his attorney, he had "become accustomed to the life of luxury while married to the star he had created and managed." Thus he was now affected financially and emotionally. They estimated that he deserved $6,000 a month in spousal support and $100,000 for his attorney fees. I couldn't imagine it. Wasn't this the man I had stood by when he went to jail? Even made his child-support payments when he was there? Did I not save him from deportation by marrying him? He had cheated on me during the most difficult time in my life and now I owed him? Ain't that a bitch.

On the plus side, I had met a new man, Fernando, who treated me better than Trino or Juan ever had. And I was finally getting properly laid.

14

Pinche Pelón

Is it raining at your house like it's raining at mine?
Does it thunder and lightning even when the sun shines?
—from "Is It Raining at Your House?"

I first saw Fernando that night at the Mirage with Erika in April of 2003, the same night I decided it was over with Juan. Fernando was working in the promotions department at Que Buena, and he was at the Mirage working an event. We made eye contact from a distance, and I was immediately attracted to him. He looked like a bit of a thug with a fully shaved head and a handsome face. That night we didn't speak, but I definitely remembered him.

I saw him again a few weeks later at a warehouse shoe-sale promotion for Que Buena. He had the fine job of taking me to the dressing room and making sure that I was all right. I felt a connection from the moment he started talking. He was so funny and charming. When I was sitting at the table signing autographs, I whispered to Rosie, "Do you see the bald-headed guy? Isn't he so cute?"

"Yeah, he's cute," she said. "But he looks like a *cholo*."

It was true. He was wearing a big old jersey, baggy jeans, and white

133

Nike Cortez. He was so different from any other guy I had ever been with, which is probably why I was so attracted to him. Something about him I couldn't get out of my mind.

The third time we saw each other was on July 16, 2003, at El Rodeo, a nightclub in Pico Rivera. My father had a performance there that night, and I went with Gus, Juan, and my sister-in-law Brenda to hang out and watch him sing. I was already pretty well known in Southern California, especially among the crowd at El Rodeo. Fernando approached me, we spoke briefly, and he said, "Look, I know you're busy, but if you could just promise me you'll dance the last song with me?"

I said, "Okay, I promise."

As the lights started to come up for last call, I was dancing with someone else, but I stopped to look around for Fernando. He was standing there, waiting to see what I was going to do. I walked toward him and called him over. We had our first dance, but afterward we lost each other in the crowd. I was a little tipsy, and as the night was coming to a close, my brothers were trying to get me in their car.

"No," I told them. "I want to talk to the bald-headed guy. I'm not leaving until I talked to the bald-headed guy."

When they saw that I wouldn't give in, Brenda went searching for him. Fernando was already in the Que Buena work van and packed up to leave. Brenda knocked on the van door and told him, "Jenni says we're not leaving until you come talk to her."

"Okay, where is she?"

Brenda brought him to me.

"Where are you going?" I asked him.

"Jack in the Box."

"Great," I said. "I'm going with you."

I jumped in his work van with him and his friend George, who was driving. The van was packed with speakers, canopies, and a whole bunch of other crap. I sat on a speaker as we drove to the Jack in the Box, which was right across the street from El Rodeo. Apparently it was where everyone went after the club let out. We were waiting in the long drive-through line when I saw my brothers Gus and Juan walking toward the van. They opened the sliding door and saw me chilling on top of the speaker.

"Get your ass out of the van, Jenni," Juan told me.

"No," I said, crossing my arms. "I'm not getting out."

We were holding up the entire line, and people started to look at Juan and me fighting in the back of the Que Buena van. Everybody seemed to be enjoying the show and didn't much care that we were causing such a backup.

When Juan got tired of arguing with me, he grabbed me and threw me in the trunk of his car. He was about to slam the lid on me when Fernando came running toward us. "Hold up!" he was yelling. "Don't shut the door." That's how Fernando first met my brothers Juan and Gus. He got me out of the trunk, and then, as usual, I got my way. My brothers let me go in the van with Fernando, but Juan said, "If you're hanging out with him tonight, we're hanging out together. You follow us to my house."

After we got our tacos, we headed out on the freeway, following Juan to his place. George was driving and Fernando was in the passenger seat. I was still in the back sitting on the speaker.

"Lose him! Come on! Lose him!" I screamed to George.

Fernando said, "You better not, George. Just keep fucking following them."

"Don't be a bitch!" I screamed. "Lose him, George!"

No matter how loud I was yelling, Fernando just kept repeating, "Just keep fucking following them, George."

Poor George didn't know what to do, but he ended up listening to

Fernando, despite my plan's being far better. We got to Juan's house and we all hung out and kept drinking. The more I talked to Fernando, the more I liked him. That night he finally got my number.

A few days later Fernando called to ask me out to dinner. I didn't want to wait to see him. "Where are you right now?" I asked.

"Pacoima."

"Good. I'm close to there. Let's just meet up now."

We met at Hansen Dam. We drove to get tacos and then went back to the dam with our food. We sat there talking for hours about everything and anything. I had never connected with anyone else the way I connected with Fernando. We understood each other. We both came from the hood. We both grew up listening to the oldies and knew every classic song that would come on the radio. I could talk to him about anything: my kids, my career, the evolution of different music genres, trends in the industry. He was smart, interesting, and sweet. Best of all, the motherfucker could make me laugh. Any guy I had dated in the past never got my sense of humor. Fuck, any guy I had dated in the past had never even had a sense of humor. With Fernando it was a whole new ball game. Before I knew it, eight hours had passed. This is it, I thought. This is the one.

And then . . . we didn't talk for a month.

It was my fault. He called me and I never called him back. I was going through such a horrible time with Juan and the divorce. It was messier than I could have imagined, and it was consuming my every moment. When I finally called Fernando, I got a message that the number was no longer in service. I called the radio station and got hold of George, who gave me Fernando's new number. That night we talked on the phone for thirteen hours straight.

We got deeper into each other's story. I told him things I'd never shared with anyone else. Something about him let me open up.

On one of our first dates we were sitting at a Norms diner and ordered our drinks. I asked for a lemonade and Fernando sang, "Lemonade, that cool refreshing drink," just like Eddie Murphy in his *Delirious* comedy routine. I loved all comedy and I used to watch that Eddie Murphy comedy routine on repeat. I knew every word. Juan López didn't get it. Trino, forget about it. But along came this guy who could quote it, with just the right inflection and at just the right time. If I could pinpoint the moment I fell in love with the motherfucker, that might have been it.

After a few weeks, he took me on the *Queen Mary* for a weekend and refused to let me pay for anything. It was so ironic. I was in the middle of a bitter divorce with Juan, who had no problem spending my money and was now demanding a big chunk of my earnings. Yet, this guy, with barely a cent to his name, would not even let me open my wallet. He opened the doors for me, pulled out the chair. He may have looked like a *cholo*, but his mother had taught him how to be a gentleman.

When we sat down to dinner, I turned to look at the ocean. The sea foam had turned electric neon blue, as though someone were shining a blacklight on it. Everyone stared in awe. Somebody explained to us that this rare phenomenon occurs when the cells and bacteria and organisms all come together in a specific way. It rarely happens on the shoreline. To this day it is one of the most interesting and beautiful sights I have ever seen. These kinds of special moments kept happening when I was with Fernando, as though the universe were telling me that I had finally found something good.

Fernando was so different from anyone else I had ever dated. He was ten years younger than me and living with his mother in a tiny house in the San Fernando Valley. He'd work a nine-to-five if he had a job, but he'd always lose it. He didn't even have a car when we first met. He'd drive around in his mom's old green Ford Escort until he blew it out one day after trying to keep up with me on the freeway.

None of that mattered to me. What mattered was that he gave me the passion and the devotion that I'd always wanted.

I had already been through so much in life, but in so many ways I was still quite innocent and inexperienced. For one, I had never smoked pot, and Fernando was something of an expert. He smoked every morning and every night. When I told him, he didn't believe me. "Come on," he said, "you're trying to tell me you grew up in Long Beach and you've never smoked weed?"

That night I smoked for the first time and I didn't feel a thing. That's how he knew I wasn't lying. He explained that nobody feels it on their first go-round. The next time we smoked, it hit me right away. I couldn't stop laughing. Everything he said became the funniest thing I'd ever heard. This was also the first night that I realized how good sex could be. It must have been a combination of the pot and my feelings for him, because that night I finally had my first orgasm. I was thirty-four years old.

I never felt more beautiful than when I was with Fernando. He was handsome and I knew he could get any girl he wanted. All of his ex-girlfriends were thin, model-looking chicks, but he would constantly say that nobody compared to me. He was always complimenting me, and whenever I would talk about losing weight, he would say, "Babe, don't change a thing. You are beautiful just as you are."

To him I wasn't an artist, I was just Jen. He loved my singing and supported me, but it was just a career to him. He loved me for the passionate, down, crazy, gangsta woman I was when the spotlight was off and it was just the two of us kicking it in the Corona house. Or when we were driving around—listening to music and talking—with no destination in mind, but all of our favorite singers bumping through the stereo. Mary Wells, Heatwave, the Delfonics, the Stylistics, Easy-E, Biggie, Tupac, Ice-T, Alejandra Guzmán, Graciela Beltrán, Chayito Valdez, Sade, Whitney Houston, Beyoncé, Alicia Keys. You name it, we listened to it. Aside from heavy metal and the dreaded *durangeunse*, no genre was off-limits. We both loved the oldies, hip-hop, jazz. Rap, reggae, rock. And I even turned the thug from Boyle Heights into a country-music fan. "Listen to the words," I would tell him. "These people know how to tell a story." Our song became Brad Paisley's recording of "Is It Raining at Your House?" We would dig into the musicians' backgrounds. We'd find out what influenced them and take inspiration from their choices. With Fernando, I finally had someone I could talk to about different ideas and directions to take in my career.

The first time he met my whole family was at Jenicka's sixth birthday party, in October of 2003. The party was at Chuck E. Cheese's, which isn't a bad place to introduce a guy to your family. It keeps things light.

Even so, my family wasn't exactly thrilled. They wanted to know what he had to offer. Whenever my mom would meet a guy I dated, she would remember who they were according to what they gave her. One guy gave her sweet bread, so she'd ask, "Where is the guy with the bread?" And when I broke up with him, she'd say, "Oh, now who is going to give me sweet bread?" A few months later I brought a carpenter. Mom was thinking, "Oh, good, he can fix my roof." She had the guy paint the house.

So when my mother met Fernando, she said, "What is he going to give me?" He wasn't working at the radio station anymore; he was working at a porn warehouse and selling the DVDs out of the back of his truck. Not exactly what Mom was looking for, I assumed. Nobody was too thrilled about my seeing him. Everyone thought I could do better, but I knew they would come around. He treated me so well and he loved *me*—not Jenni the singer, but Jenni the person. Eventually they saw that too. You couldn't deny it.

Plus, he was fun and charismatic. He won everyone over, especially my kids. The Riveras like anyone who can kick back and have a good time. That was Fernie (the nickname they all use for him). My sister would say, "Hanging with Fernie is like hanging with you. You know you're going to get in trouble, but you know you'll never get caught."

After about four or five months Fernie was everyone's favorite, but I still hadn't met any of his family or friends. It started to piss me off. "Are you hiding me?" I would ask him. "Are you fucking another girl?"

"No, babe. It's just not safe for people to know we're together. I live in the ghetto. I have to think about my mom. You have to understand."

When I did meet his mother, I adored her from the first second I laid eyes on her. She is an incredible woman. She raised two sons on her own on a minimum-wage job. Her husband left her when Fernando was four, and after that she never had another man. She attends a two-hour mass every single morning, and she can put together a thrift-store outfit and make it look as if it came from a high-end department store. I called her *suegra* (mother-in-law) from the beginning. We shared a special bond, and I would call her to talk things through or ask her for guidance and prayers. I would also go to visit her on my own. I just loved being in her company.

One day I guess some men saw me walking out of her house. That night, at three in the morning, five men came knocking at her door. "We want to see Jenni!" they were yelling. "My wife is dying and her last wish is to meet Jenni!"

Fernando was at a friend's house three blocks away when his mother called him. He sprinted to her house and found the five drunk men on his mother's front stoop. He told them to get the hell out of there and then he called me, pissed, to tell me what had happened.

"You see? You live up in your gated community, up in your la-la land, and I'm down here dealing with all the shit. Do you see?"

After that I was much more careful. Together we decided to keep our relationship private. He never wanted the attention and ran from a camera whenever he saw one in our presence. I wanted something to myself, something that the media could not pick apart. Because such a huge part of my life was becoming public, it felt good to have this privacy, this one element of my world that was my very own.

About six months into our relationship Fernando got an apartment in Van Nuys, though he could barely afford it. He said he wanted us to have a place where we could be alone. We would sneak out of the balcony in the back so his neighbors wouldn't see us. I had a key, and sometimes I would go to clean for him, leave him a cooked meal, and take his laundry back to my house so I could do it for him. One time I was climbing over the back balcony carrying his laundry bag as if I were Santa Claus. As I was lifting my leg over the railing, I heard a man's voice say, "Jenni? Jenni Rivera?" It was the trash collector, who recognized me even though I had on sweats, a ball cap, and no makeup. "Yes," I told him as I waved and smiled awkwardly, "it's me."

That night Fernando called. "Babe, thank you! But what did you do to my bong?"

"Your what?"

"The glass thing that was on the counter."

"Oh, the flower vase! That was the dirtiest flower vase I have ever seen. It took me forever to get all the dirt out of it."

He loved that I was this tough ghetto girl from Long Beach, but I also had this innocent, naive side that needed to be shown the difference between a bong and a flower vase. It gave our relationship a spark.

When my career started to take off in the fall of 2005, I was traveling a lot more and performing every weekend. I couldn't stand to be apart from him, and my kids were crazy about him too. I asked him to move into the house in Corona with us and to join me on the road. That's when the true craziness began.

Fernando and I are so much alike. We are both incredibly passionate, stubborn, loving, prideful—and neither of us is known for backing down. Throughout our relationship, we loved and fought with the same level of intensity. When things were good, they were really good. There was no couple you'd rather be around. But when things were bad, they got ugly. I had been so hurt and broken down by Trino and Juan that with this relationship I was determined that it wouldn't happen again. I was a bit hardened and I wanted to maintain the upper hand a lot of the time. But Fernando wasn't going to let me step all over him. If I screamed at him or called him a name, he would tell me, "Don't talk to me like that. I'll sleep under the freeway if I have to, but don't talk to me like that."

Our fights usually started over something small and stupid, but they would escalate into huge battles. We never hit each other, but we would kick down doors and break furniture. We'd get thrown out of hotels for screaming in the hallways and for wrecking the rooms. Anyone who was nearby would quickly find an excuse to leave in order to escape the drama. All of a sudden everyone would have to go to the 7-Eleven or the hotel bar.

In every single fight, neither of us would back down and apologize. He'd pack a bag and leave for two or three weeks. I would usually be the one to reach out and call for some lame reason. "You left your white T-shirt here," I'd say. "Are you going to come get it?" Or: "If you're hungry, I'm cooking tonight." That was my form of an apology, and he knew it. He would meet me halfway by saying he was sorry first, and then we would be back on as if nothing had happened.

When we were on these breaks, we would inevitably meet other people, give out our numbers, or go on a few dates. But when we were back on and one of those random numbers called, it would start another world war and lead to another period of our not talking. So began our endless cycle of "break up to make up."

I never stopped loving him through any of it. When we were not speaking, I would be crying onstage and nobody knew why, but it was almost always for Fernando. I would often dedicate songs to *mi pinche pelón* (my baldy), and nobody knew who it was. This was the one relationship that I wanted to make work so badly, and I thought if I protected it from the media, then we might have a shot, so I never talked about him in the press. Of course, I talked about everything else, though . . .

15

Two More Years

Te prometo no dejar ninguna huella
ninguna evidencia de que yo estuve ahí.

(*I promise to leave no trace
no evidence that I was there.*)
—from "De Contrabando"

My famous line to my family and to Fernando was always "two more years." I would tell them, "I'm just going to do this for two more years, and then I'll stay home and be normal." But I guess "normal" was never in the cards for me.

In 2003 and 2004 I recorded about eight songs in English because I wanted to do an English album. My father said, "You don't want the Latinos to think, 'Oh, look, she got famous and now she is leaving us.'" I followed his advice and instead worked on my next album, *Parrandera, Rebelde y Atrevida* (A Party Girl, Rebellious and Bold). When it was released in October of 2005, it immediately hit the Top 20 on *Billboard*'s Top Latin Albums chart. In weeks it went gold and then platinum. I got a contract to sing at the Kodak Theatre in Hollywood.

No other female Mexican artist had ever done that. I said to myself, "Okay, I'll do the Kodak and then I'll get to the Gibson and then I'll be done. I don't need to prove anything after that. Just give me two more years . . ."

I did an interview with El Piolín on the Los Angeles radio station La Nueva. We were discussing my album and my upcoming concert, and after talking about some of my new songs and lyrics, El Piolín asked me who I would prefer to record a song with if I had the choice, Graciela Beltrán or Mariana Seoane. I was always the girl who didn't hold back. If an interviewer asked me a question, I answered honestly. I'm sure any publicist would have told me to say, "I love them both, I can't choose." Instead I spoke from the heart and said, "From those choices, I would pick Graciela Beltrán."

"Why?"

"Because for me, she has more talent."

"What does Mariana have?"

"I don't know. I think she has *palancas* [connections], people who help her push her career forward."

That comment started a huge media scandal. Obviously, Mariana heard about it. A few days later my brother Lupillo went to do an interview with El Piolín, and the station called me and put me on air to comment on Lupillo's interview. But in reality they had a surprise for me; Mariana Seoane was waiting on the air. She was upset with me. I said, "Look, I never said you didn't have talent. I think you obviously have charisma to be in this business, but you also have people who have supported you and helped launch you. That doesn't mean it's anything bad. It would have been great if I had that." Nevertheless, she was offended. Off the air we agreed to meet to talk it out. I thought we had put it behind us after that, but I was wrong.

Shortly after that, I was invited to sing the national anthem at "Viva Dodgers Night." Since I have always been a huge baseball fan, it was a great honor for me. The show *El Gordo y la Flaca* called and asked if I could join them live on the show the next Monday to discuss my singing of the national anthem. I said of course. That Monday I was on my way to the show when I got a call telling me that Mariana Seoane was also live out of Miami on the show. I was surprised, but I was not going to back out of the interview. Lili Estephan and a guest host were doing the show that day since El Gordo de Molina was on vacation.

Once again, they asked me about my comment about Mariana on El Piolín's show. I defended my statement once more, but this time Mariana came back on and said I also had *palancas* because I had my brother Lupillo. I responded that I was the one sitting down giving the interview, not my brother. I told her that I recorded, I managed my own image, and I gave my own interviews. Nobody had ever played my music just because I was Lupillo's sister. What I couldn't see, because I didn't have a monitor, was that while I was talking, Mariana was mocking me on-screen. I only had a camera in front of me. But the damage was done because my fans saw what she did. Then, all of a sudden, my image on the monitor scrambled and went to a blur. I was told that we had lost the satellite connection.

My fans went crazy. They all thought it was intentional, and so did I. Chiquis was the most upset of all. "Why would they do that to you, Mom?" she kept asking. Everywhere I went the reporters wanted to hear my reaction about being "taken off the air" on *El Gordo y la Flaca*. Obviously I wasn't going to let the whole thing die without getting the last word.

A month later I went to Miami to promote my record live on *El Gordo y la Flaca*. This time El Gordo de Molina was there. They apologized left and right about what had happened with the satellite the last time. I told them I would like to dedicate a song to whoever had anything to do with cutting me off the air. I sang the verse: *Este verso es pa' tu, abuela, y los que llevan tu sangre. Agarrados de la mano, chingen todos a su madre* (This verse is for you, your grandma, and your bloodline. Hold each other's hands, and go fuck your mother). Then I stood up, took off my microphone, placed it on the table, and walked off the set.

"Did you really just do that? Did I just see what I think I saw?" I could barely hear a word Jazmin, the talent representative from my label, was saying. I had just cursed *El Gordo y la Flaca* off, live, on the air. Nobody had ever done that. Ever. I told Jazmin, "Ah, well, I'm sure I'll never be asked back on."

Had I gone too far? Did they deserve it? Was that a big career mistake? The truth is, I didn't care. No self-respecting chick from the West Side of Long Beach would care about any of that. Because no self-respecting chick from the West Side of Long Beach would ever worry about what was right, what was wise, and what was responsible when it came to defending her honor.

This event made me "the infamous Jenni Rivera." The media talked about it every chance they could. Some people wanted me to retract my statement and apologize, but there was no way I was going to do that. I didn't feel any remorse for what I had done, so I was not going to be a phony or a hypocrite. My fan base, instead of abandoning me, only grew stronger and more supportive.

The night of my concert at the Kodak, October 14, 2005, I found out that it was sold out. As I pulled up to the theater, Hollywood Boulevard was swamped. As I looked at the lines of people wearing Jenni Rivera T-shirts, I got choked up.

"Can you believe it?" I said to nobody in particular. "The nerd from the LBC sold out the motherfucking Kodak." Not only did I sell out the motherfucking Kodak, that night the theater had the highest alcohol sales ever reported. To me that was the greatest achievement of all. Ticket sales are important, of course, but to promoters, the alcohol sales are just as important, if not more. That is how they make the bulk of their money, and so the artists who have high alcohol sales are the most beneficial to sign. And in that respect, my fans never disappointed.

To this day I still say my concert at the Kodak was my most memorable. It was the first time I sang in a theater that big and that prestigious. Soon after, I got a contract to sing at the Gibson, which had been my goal for so long.

"Okay," I kept saying. "I'll do the Gibson and then the Staples and then I'll retire. Two more years."

But then "the impossible" happened. In the spring of 2006 I got my first big gig in Mexico, at a *palenque* in Guadalajara. (In Mexico, a *palenque* is a place where both cockfights and concerts are held, and in my opinion, it is also the best place to perform.) "De Contrabando," one of the songs on my new album, had hit it big in Mexico, and all of a sudden I was known throughout the entire country. Many people told me that a singer who was not born on Mexican soil could never break into that market. People in the industry told me it was impossible, so you can imagine how excited I was to be proving them wrong once again. Though I will admit I was also a little nervous, since times were rough in Mexico, and several regional Mexican artists had recently been kidnapped or killed.

I asked my brother Juan if he had any friends who could protect us. Juan always knows the people you need to know. When we arrived at the airport in Mexico, we were greeted by several armored cars driven by government officials, and they brought us to the *palenque*.

My band and I were set up in the small circle in the middle of the *palenque*, and thousands of fans surrounded us. The closest fans were less than ten feet from me, and they were handing me tequila shots throughout the night as they sang along to my songs. The energy was so high and so contained, and when I finished that concert, I was buzzing on alcohol and adrenaline.

Outside, the caravan of armored cars was waiting for us. As we drove away, we opened the moon roof in the car. I asked one of the government officials to let me see his gun. For some reason he did, and without hesitating, I stood up and shot the gun in the night air. Between shots I heard the government official say to my brother, "What the fuck is she doing? I could be arrested."

Juan asked the obvious question: "Well, why the fuck did you give her the gun?"

The next night I was scheduled to sing at another *palenque* in Uruapán, 160 miles southeast of Guadalajara. That morning we heard rumors that something was going to happen to me.

Juan said, "Let's just cancel the gig."

"I can't do that."

"Is it worth it?"

"It's not about the money. People are coming to see me. I can't let them down. Will you go with me?"

"Well, shit, I don't have a choice."

We drove from Guadalajara to Uruapán with thirty cop cars surrounding us. I was sitting in the middle between Juan and Hector, Chiquis's fiancé, who served as one of my protectors. As we approached the crowded venue, Juan said, "Hector, if any shots get fired, we fall on my sister."

"All right," he said. "I got you."

We pulled up to the doors and all I saw were machine guns everywhere.

Juan hugged me. "I don't know if anything is going to happen tonight. But if we are going, we are going to ride together, all right?"

"All right, Brother. Just don't bitch out."

Nothing happened that night at the *palenque*, but we were still on edge when we got to our hotel. Hector and Juan told me they were going to sleep outside my door. I went to bed, and they decided that they were going to get drunk so if anything happened, they wouldn't feel it. I woke up the next morning and they were hammered.

"Oh, this is great. I got two dumbass drunk security guards taking care of me."

"Did anything happen?" Juan asked.

"No."

"Then shut the fuck up."

16

Speaking Out

Levanto mis manos aunque no tengo fuerzas.

(*I lift up my hands to you*
even when my strength is failing.)
—from "Levanto Mis Manos"

In January of 2006 Rosie saw Trino for the first time in nine years. She was sitting at Norms restaurant in Lakewood with Gladyz when she spotted him a few tables away. She froze. She couldn't speak, and Gladyz kept asking her what was wrong. Then Trino looked over and locked eyes with Rosie. He froze too. But then in an instant he stood up, put money on the table, and left, passing right by their table as he headed for the door. Rosie didn't take a breath until he was outside.

By that time Gladyz was screaming at her, "Are you going to tell me what the hell is going on?"

"It was Trino," she finally managed to say. "Go get his plates." Gladyz ran out into the parking lot, and that's when Rosie went to the pay phone to call me.

The first words out of her mouth were "Sister, I'm sorry. I am so stupid. I failed you."

"What are you talking about?" I asked. "What happened?"

"I just saw Trino and I didn't do anything."

"Where are you?"

"At the Norms two miles from Mom's house."

"Was he with anyone?"

"Yes, he was with a woman."

"Dora?"

"No. Someone else."

"That bastard. I'm sure he's cheating on her. Did he look the same?"

"It looked like he had some plastic surgeries to his face. But it was him. I knew by his eyes."

Gladyz came back in and told Rosie she couldn't get his plates. He sped away too fast.

Rosie started to cry. "I didn't do anything. All of these years I dreamed of what I would do, and I didn't do anything."

"Listen to me," I told her. "You did exactly the right thing. It's good that you saw him. You didn't fail me. We are going to catch the moth- erfucker. Are you ready to talk about it?"

Speaking out about sexual abuse was so taboo back then, espe- cially in the Mexican American community. People used to turn a blind eye and keep their mouths shut because they were too embar- rassed or too scared of what might happen to them. Up until 2006 I had never spoken about Trino and the allegations against him, but it was always on my mind. I knew that one day I would get a sign that it was time. That day came in 2006, shortly after Rosie had seen Trino at the diner. Chiquis came home from high school and told me, "Mom, four out of five of my friends have been sexually abused. I want to help them, but I don't know how."

I asked Chiquis the same question I asked Rosie: "Are you ready to speak about it publicly? That is what will help them and millions of other girls and women." Chiquis, Rosie, and Jacqie all agreed that they were ready. I contacted talk-show host Charytín about doing a special with us. I trusted her and I knew she would handle it with grace and sensitivity.

Everyone was advising me against doing the show. They said my career would be over. I told them I didn't care if I lost it all. I'd been poor before, I could do it again. To me this issue was too important not to talk about publicly. Somebody had to be the voice and let girls out there know that they were not alone and they had the power to speak up and speak out. I told Rosie, Chiquis, and Jacqie that they could be that voice. God gave us a platform so they could help others. It was the only way I could make sense of what had happened to my sister and my daughters.

At the end of March 2006, Rosie, Chiquis, Jacqie, and I sat down with Charytín in our Corona house to talk openly about the sexual abuse they had suffered. This was the first time that any of them had done a TV interview, and it was on such a difficult topic. I could tell that they were all nervous, and I was too. But I could not show it. I had to be brave so they could be brave. I had to be fearless so they could be fearless.

Once we were on that show, the news started to spread like wildfire. So did the backlash. People said I was only doing it for publicity and attention. They said I was hurting my sister and my daughters. They said we were lying. I didn't give a fuck. I knew in my heart we were doing the right thing.

In April, K-Love, a national radio network, invited us on. We did a long interview, and the calls started to come in from fans giving us tips or telling us where they might have seen Trino. Then a lady called in and requested that she remain anonymous and that her voice not be put on air. Fear was in her voice. She made us promise that we would never reveal her name and that her husband and children would never find out that she had spoken to us. I promised her I would keep her safe.

"He is my neighbor," she said. "I know him." She gave us his address and some more information about him that let me know that she was telling the truth. She was our first big key.

Our second big key, an FBI agent, called in just a few minutes later, and he also asked that he not be put on air.

"I shouldn't be doing this," he said, "but your story affected me so deeply. I want to help you."

With Trino's address and the FBI agent on our side, we soon had Trino backed against the wall.

On April 22, 2006, the FBI agent called Rosie and said, "You have seen him. You can identify him."

I was on the road, traveling to my next concert, when Rosie called me.

"You see?" I told her. "It all worked for the good. God has given this to you."

"We're going to get him," she told me. She was in the back of the FBI van with Mom. They were driving through Corona to Trino's house.

"Are you scared?"

"Yeah."

"Don't be scared. He's the motherfucker that should be scared. Poor motherfucker doesn't even know what's coming."

Rosie later told me how it all went down. He was outside watering his garden when they pulled up. They approached him and put him in handcuffs.

His wife, Dora, started to lose it. "Please don't take him!" she cried. "He's innocent."

Then his eight-year-old daughter, Diana, ran out of the house and sobbed, "Don't take my daddy! Please don't take my daddy!"

That part broke Rosie's heart. As the cops led him to a police car, he was only ten or fifteen feet away from Rosie and Mom. They could see him, but he had no idea they were behind those van windows. They told me how he looked so small and powerless, and Rosie said she felt as if the roles had been reversed. He was the one in chains, while she was now free.

They drove two or three blocks in silence, and then Mom and Rosie started to shriek and cry tears of joy. The FBI agent kept repeating, "Glory to God. Glory to God."

Rosie called me again and said the three words I had been waiting to hear for nine years: "We got him."

"Fuck yeah!" I screamed.

"But poor little Diana. She lost her daddy."

"Sister, don't forget. My kids lost their daddy too. And what if he is hurting Diana too? You are probably saving her life."

Later we found out that the FBI had been videotaping him and they interviewed all of his neighbors. One of the neighbors said, "I don't talk to him. And my daughter is not allowed to play with his daughter."

The FBI agent gave Rosie the handcuffs he had used to arrest Trino.

A few weeks later Rosie was going to sing her first solo in church. "Will you be there?" she asked me.

I wouldn't have missed it for anything. She sang a song of victory with tears streaming down her face. I was crying too as she walked off the stage and handed the cuffs to me. I hugged my baby doll so tightly then. I was so grateful that God had given her such peace and helped her to find her voice and her path back to light.

In the parking lot I said to her, "Sister, you know how to perform. You are good onstage!"

"It was an altar," she reminded me.

"Whatever. It looked like a stage to me. And you had presence."

"I learned it from you."

"Can I keep these?" I asked, holding up the handcuffs. "I want to use them for the cover of my book."

"Of course, those are yours. You risked your career for us. You worked to give us justice. Those are yours."

17

Look at Me

Mírame, no soy la misma de antes
esta sonrisa es por alguien que quiero a morir.

(*Look at me, I'm not the same as before*
this smile is for someone I love to death.)
—from "Mírame"

The day that we caught Trino, April 22, 2006, was so emotional.
It was a relief and a victory because I knew there was finally going
to be justice. But it was also so difficult because he was, after all, my
children's father. Despite what he had done, Chiquis and Jacqie kept
saying, "We don't want Dad to be hurt."

Three days after the arrest we went to his arraignment, and I saw
him for the first time in nine years. He never looked at me, but I didn't
take my eyes off of him. He wore a prison jumpsuit. His hair was cut
shorter. He had done something to his face, but I couldn't figure out
what it was that looked different. He didn't display a hint of remorse.
I was angry, sad, and full of guilt and shame. Because he appeared

without a lawyer, we had to go back on May 2. He was held on a million-dollar bail because he was considered a flight risk.

After the first arraignment date, Chiquis, who was almost twenty-one, said to me, "Let's not do this. If he says he's sorry, can we forget about it?"

"Mija, we cannot let him go just like that," I responded. "There has to be justice for you, for your sister, your Tía Rosie, and all the girls out there who are victims of this abuse. And I want you to one day have a relationship with your father. This is the only way that is going to happen." Because Chiquis had been called a liar so many times by Trino's family, I couldn't let that go on for the rest of her life. I knew that taking him to trial was the right thing to do.

I did my best to stay strong for my daughters, but I was a mess inside. I confided in Rosie, "I can't handle everything right now. I need you to talk to the lawyers, the detectives, and the police officers. Can you do that?" She nodded that she could.

A year earlier, in a promotion by a diamond company, the tagline was "Women of the world, raise your right hand." The idea was that you didn't have to wait for a man to buy you a rock, you could buy one yourself and wear it on your right ring finger. So I'd bought myself a gorgeous, large diamond as a symbol that I was independent and in love with myself.

When Trino's trial was about to start, I took the ring off, handed it to Rosie, and said, "Sister, I'm giving you this ring for strength and support. Finally you are going to have justice and peace." We called it the Victory Ring and she wore it throughout the trial.

The trial lasted nearly fourteen months. The courthouse was always packed. All of Trino's family was on one side, and all of my family was on the other. I petitioned to bar cameras from the courtroom, but I could not prevent the journalists from being there since it was a public place.

As my popularity grew, so did the media's interest in my personal life, and the trial was front and center. The two largest Spanish-language TV networks, Univision and Telemundo, reported every detail. On top of it all, I also had to go to court with my other ex-husband, Juan, who was demanding I pay him even more spousal support. Our divorce was still not finalized. On June 9, 2006, nine years to the day when I had married Juan, a judge in the Riverside family-law court decided I was to pay only $20,000 to his attorney, instead of the $100,000 that he'd asked for. He would get nothing else from me, and the spousal support that I had paid for three years (which was nothing close to the $6,000 a month he wanted) was to end. In fact, the judge decided that Juan owed me due to overpayments during those three years. Juan could try to fight for the house in Corona, but doing so would be costly and time-consuming. Instead, we decided to settle that out of court and finally put the legal battle behind us.

Once we were done fighting, Juan and I grew to be friends. We had two children together and some beautiful memories from our eight-year relationship. I decided to focus on that. He was nothing like Trino. He was a great father to Jenicka and Johnny, and I would always love him for that. He moved into an apartment less than five minutes from my home in Corona, and he saw the kids often.

On June 3, 2006, my song "De Contrabando" hit number one on the *Billboard* Regional Mexican airplay list. I was getting gigs in Mexico almost every weekend, and I booked my first concert at the Gibson Amphitheatre for August 5. I was excited and grateful to God to have something to look forward to besides wanting to strangle Trino with my bare hands.

I informed my manager, Gabo, that no matter what offer came along, we had to work around the trial. I would not miss a single day.

All of my brothers cleared their calendars as well so that we could be there for our sister and my daughters.

We had to go to court about once a month, and each time the courtroom was packed. Every single person from Trino's extended family was there crying and shouting that he was innocent, despite all of the evidence and testimony indicating that he was guilty of the most disgusting and horrifying shit. I understand why they didn't want to admit the truth. The truth was so fucking ugly. But it was there. Plain and simple. And sickening.

The day that Rosie and Chiquis gave their testimony tore my heart open all over again. I can't imagine what it must have been like for them. Before Rosie took the stand, she was nervous and ashamed. "How am I going to say these words in front of my father?" she asked me. "In front of my brothers? And with Trino sitting right there?"

Lupe told her, "Just look at me, Sister. Whatever you do, don't look at him. Look at me."

"I can't," she answered. "It's too embarrassing. It's going to hurt you too much."

"I can take it, Rosie. I will be fine. Look at me," Lupe kept repeating.

Rosie did as Lupe said. She looked right at him as she narrated the details of her trauma. Tears streamed down all of our faces. Chiquis waited outside since she wasn't allowed to be in the courtroom when Rosie gave her testimony. We took a recess, and before Chiquis was set to take the stand, she told me she wasn't sure if she could go through with it. I sat with her on the bench in the hallway and said, "You can do this, princess. You can do this for all the other little girls who have suffered. For all the women who are afraid to speak out. You can be their voice. I am here for you."

Her testimony was crucial to the case. Without it, Trino could possibly have walked free. I reminded her that we couldn't let that happen. She bravely took the stand and spoke about what her father had done to her since she was eight years old. She had to take breaks, but she got through it all with such strength. Much of what she said echoed Rosie's testimony. The way it started, how it escalated, the threats he made, where and when he did it.

With each incident that they described, I would ask myself, "Where was I? Why couldn't I stop it? Why couldn't I protect them?" The guilt pressing down on my chest was unbearable, but I had to keep my head up. I had to show Rosie and Chiquis that I was a source of strength that they could lean on.

Aside from their testimony, there were the medical records, which could simply not be denied. Yet Trino and his family did still deny it. In the elevators and the hallways, Trino's family would say, "You are fucking whores and fucking liars." I wanted to beat them down, but we were in a courthouse and I knew I could get arrested and not be allowed to attend the trial with my daughters and sister. I refused to let my temper get the best of me.

That didn't mean I wasn't threatening. When Trino's family was with us in the elevators, I told them, "What the fuck are you looking at? Turn around. Face the fucking wall." When they called me a whore, I shot back, "At least I'm not ugly."

On the morning of August 5, 2006, I was preparing for my concert at the Gibson. The same place where I had seen so many of my idols perform. The same stage where Vicente Fernández brought me up to sing in 2001 and then told the audience that I had the talent to make it.

As I was getting ready, my managers called me and told me we were sold out and I was the first female *banda* artist to sell out the Gibson. I started to cry. When I took the stage on that unforgettable summer night, the tears continued. I was crying tears of joy for all of my blessings. Tears of pain for all of my heartache. Tears of gratitude for the thousands of fans who sang along with me, cheering for me, shouting out that they loved me, every chance they got. Amid the nightmare I was living, it was a dream come true.

In October 2006 Trino posted the million-dollar bail. I have no idea how the asshole came up with the money, but we thought for sure he was going to flee. Instead, he showed up at the next court date in a suit and tie. Now that he was no longer in a prison jumpsuit, Trino appeared confident and cocky. As he walked out of the courtroom during a recess, he looked at my brother Lupillo and smiled. My son Michael, who looked to all of his uncles as father figures, lunged at Trino, the man he did not consider a father at all. Michael punched Trino in the face, and in seconds an all-out street fight broke out in the courtroom. At least forty Riveras and Maríns were punching, pulling hair, and banging heads. Every cop in the courthouse ran in to break it up, and though they had the right to arrest us all, they let us off with a warning.

By the grace of God, my brother Juan was late that day and arrived twenty minutes after the fight. If he had been there, I know he would have gone crazy and beat the shit out of half of Trino's family. Most likely he'd have been taken to jail. When he did arrive, the court officials said that he couldn't sit in the courtroom that day. "We can't have a man of your size in here after what happened today," they explained.

After that fight, security was tripled. The families had to be escorted in separately. We didn't ride in the elevators or enter and exit the courthouse together any longer.

The trial finally concluded in May of 2007. Trino's attorney, Richard Poland, stood in front of the jury and told them that I had influenced Rosie and Chiquis to make up such lies because it would boost my career. He said that back in 1997, when we first filed a complaint against Trino, I was just starting out in the music business, and he suggested that I hoped to jump-start my career with a criminal case against my ex-husband. "Jenni Rivera was selling cassettes on Atlantic Avenue when this whole thing started," he said. "Now she is a successful recording artist." I wanted to bash his head against the fucking wall. But I sat there, trying to remain calm and reminding myself that he had to make this shit up since he had nothing else to go on. "What can be worse than being a child molester?" he asked the jury. "Maybe being accused as a child molester."

The district attorney representing my family drew his closing arguments from the facts instead of making shit up out of thin air: "This is such a textbook example of what a sexual-molestation case is all about. He took advantage of the repeated access he had to Rosie and Chiquis because he was a family member, and he preyed on their sexual inexperience and embarrassment. They were 'easy targets,' and because they were so young and so threatened, it took years for them to summon the courage to speak out. Trinidad Marín is a predator," the district attorney assured the jurors, "and highly deserving of the highest stigma of sexual molestation."

After the jurors left to begin deliberation, a heated verbal fight broke out between my family and Trino's. With so many security guards and cops around it never came to blows. But if it had, I can assure you there would have been bloodshed and broken bones that day.

May 9, 2007. We sat in court awaiting the decision. My family was nervous. What would we do if the motherfucker got off? I knew God would not let it happen. He couldn't possibly let this monster walk free.

The foreman stepped to the microphone. We held each other's hands as one by one we heard the counts read off.

"On the count of continual sexual abuse of a child, we find the defendant . . . guilty."

His family began to cry. My family took a deep breath, waiting to hear more.

"On the count of lewd acts with a child under fourteen, we find the defendant . . . guilty."

More tears. More deep breaths.

"On the count of aggravated assault on a child under fourteen, we find the defendant . . . guilty."

We held each other's hands and sat in stunned silence as the foreman continued. The jury found Trino guilty of eight of the nine counts against him.

We watched the officers handcuff him. We watched as his family cried. My heart broke for them. It was not their fault. They were his victims as well.

My family sat there breathing huge, heavy sighs of relief and waiting for what would come next. The judge said, "We are going to escort the Riveras out first." We all walked out silently, still in shock. We walked to the elevator and nobody was speaking. The elevator doors closed. We all looked at each other. It was the only moment in the history of the Rivera family that nobody could speak. For nine years we had dreamed of that day. For nine years we had been chasing Trino down. Nine years and justice finally prevailed. There was nothing to say. Then Rosie started to scream. I joined her. Soon we were all screaming and crying. The sounds of relief and disbelief echoed off the elevator walls. Then the doors opened and we had to face the cameras outside. They snapped a photo of Rosie and me, and when it was published, it brought tears to my eyes. She looked so happy and free for the first time in a long while.

We had to wait six weeks for the sentencing hearing. During that time we didn't talk about the case or Trino. We were nervous because it was all in the hands of the judge and jury, but we decided to trust in God and His divine judgment.

On June 20 we went back to the court for Trino's sentencing. Both Rosie and Chiquis were given the opportunity to speak to Trino. Rosie spoke first. She did not directly address Trino because she was afraid she would break down. She spoke to the entire courtroom: "I lost my innocence when I was eight years old. From that moment forward I lost my trust in men, in myself, and in the world. I cannot say what a proper sentence would be in this case. I don't know what a person's childhood is worth." She continued, "I could no longer look my niece in the eyes because of the horrible guilt I felt. If I had spoke out about the abuse when it happened, this may never have happened to Chiquis."

"This is not your fault," the judge told her. "This is his crime, not yours. You are not responsible for anything that happened."

Rosie nodded. "Thank you," she told the judge before sitting back down.

When Chiquis spoke, she looked right at her father. "We didn't have to be here," she told him. "If you would have just said you were sorry, we wouldn't have needed a court case. I just wanted you to tell everyone that I'm not a liar." Trino refused to look at her. Chiquis continued anyway, "I want you to know that I love you. And all this time I wanted you to tell me that you loved me too." I thought he was going to look at her then. I thought he would at least have a shred of humanity in his heart to acknowledge his daughter's bravery and love. Instead he turned his head from her and rolled his motherfucking eyes. I almost lost my shit. But I held myself back. I knew I had to let the law deliver his punishment.

Michael also spoke. He was only five when Trino became a fugitive from the law. Now nearly ten years later, he finally had the chance to speak to his father. "My real reason for standing here is to say good-bye," he told Trino. "I never got to say that before. And that is all."

Trino was given a minimum of thirty-one years to life without the possibility of parole. He was led out of the courthouse in handcuffs as his family sobbed tears of grief, while my family shed tears of justice and relief. I always say that Trino's conviction on May 9 was my Mother's Day gift and his sentencing on June 20 was my Father's Day gift.

A few weeks after Trino was incarcerated, my brother Juan was contacted by some people underground. They offered to have Trino taken out in prison. It would cost $15,000. All I had to do was say the word and he would be taken care of. I couldn't do it. I couldn't have that on my conscience. And I couldn't do that to my kids either. I was holding out hope that my three oldest children would one day have a relationship with their father. I assured them all that whenever they wanted to see their father, I would drive them there. Trino said that he wanted to see Jacqie and Michael, but he refused to see Chiquis. He was still calling her a liar.

Once a piece of shit, always a piece of shit.

We decided that we couldn't let him continue to hurt Chiquis. So until he agrees to see all of them, he will see none of them.

18

I Will Bring You Home

When you're lost and you're alone and you can't get
back again
I will find you, darling, and I will bring you home.
—from "By Your Side"

Throughout the trial with Trino, I was quietly dealing with a situation that I have not ever spoken about publicly. As it was unfolding, I didn't confide in my family or friends. Only later did I tell my loved ones about the intense roller coaster I was riding with Fernando as I was trying to navigate my career, my family, and the pain of the trial.

Fernando and I had about a thousand bullshit breakups. We couldn't live with each other yet couldn't live without each other either. But in one big breakup in the summer of 2006, we stopped talking for almost six months. I couldn't deal with the constant fights and instability anymore. In addition to the awful situation with Trino, I was still going through a trial with Juan to settle our divorce, not to mention working nonstop and raising five kids as a single mother. I loved Fernando passionately, but I could only take so much. I would

169

cry in bed at night thinking that I had lost the only true love I had ever known. I never cried for Trino or Juan that way. I had never had that feeling in the pit of my stomach and the ache in my heart with them or anyone else. Fernando and I didn't speak for six months, but during the trial I was so overwhelmed. I needed my best friend and soul mate to lean on. I couldn't take it anymore, so I called him.

We got back together once again, but soon I realized he was no longer the man I had known before. He started acting crazy. He accused me of sleeping around. Then he would tell me that my brothers and I were trying to kill him. Something had happened to him during the six months in which I hadn't seen him. I thought he had schizophrenia or some kind of chemical imbalance. People around me said he was behaving as though he was on meth. I started to research his symptoms and realized that they were right. The paranoia, the rapid weight loss, the mood swings, the hyperactivity. I confronted him about it, and instead of denying it, he admitted everything. But he also told me he was going to stop and that he could do it on his own. I knew better.

I called his mother and told her what was going on. It was not an easy phone call to make. We had grown close and I cared for her so much. I didn't want to worry her, but I didn't want to hide the truth from her. She obviously knew something was wrong with her son, but she had no clue what meth was. I revealed everything I knew about the drug and the effects of it.

"What do I do?" she asked.

"We have to get him to a rehab. It's the only way to help him get right."

I kept trying to talk to him about different centers, but he didn't want to hear it. He insisted he would get better on his own. He would disappear for a week or two and then come back. He'd say he was clean, that he had gotten a job, but then a day later I could tell he was back on it. I cannot be in this relationship, I thought. But I also could not leave him.

When I didn't know what else to do, I contacted two of his friends: Carnalillo, a DJ from Que Buena, and George, the guy who was at the club when Fernando and I first met. We were going to lure him into a trap to take him to a center. But he figured it out before we were able to put the plan into action.

One day his mom begged him to go, and finally he gave in to her. She drove him to a facility in South Central LA and checked him in at about 7:00 p.m. He met the staff and the other patients. Soon after it was time for bed. They put him in a room with eight other guys. One guy was pacing back and forth from one end of the room to the other. Fernando sat in bed and watched him for a few hours, then stood up and decided he couldn't take it. This was not for him. He got out of his bed and put his shoes on. The guy who was pacing back and forth tried to get him to stay.

"You can do it, man," the guy told Fernando. "Don't give up. I know you can do it."

Fernando walked past him and right out of the facility and headed in what he thought was the direction home. He walked all of South Central at two in the morning with seventy-five cents in his pocket. He called me from a pay phone, but I did not hear my phone ringing. He somehow made it to a friend's house miles from the facility. That friend brought him back to his mother's house.

"I'm sorry. I couldn't stay at that place," he explained to us. "It was worse than county jail. I can kick this by myself. I promise."

It was a promise he could never keep. The meth had already taken its hold on him. He sank further and further into a black hole. His weight dropped to ninety pounds; he was sleeping wherever he could find a couch. For a while he was sleeping on a park bench in Hollywood. He was doing anything he could to get his hands on some money to buy more meth. He would call me at five in the morning, wide awake, and tell me about all the people who were after him. I felt helpless. Nothing is worse than watching someone you love destroy himself while you can do nothing to stop him.

I was running out of ideas. And I couldn't take the madness anymore.

I read up on how to deal with someone on meth and how to help him get better. All of the experts advised that you have to let the addict spiral and hit rock bottom. You cannot keep letting him back into the house or back into your life. As cruel as it may seem, the most loving action you can take toward an addict is to stop contact with him. I had to walk away from my soul mate and my best friend when he was at his weakest moment. I hoped that Fernando might clean himself up if he knew that he was going to lose me for good, but I knew that there is no reasoning with someone who is that far gone. All sense of logic had left him. This was not the man I had known. His light was beginning to fade, and the only thing I could do was pray for the Lord to help him find it again.

The next few months were so brutal, and I was constantly worrying about Fernando. I called his mother almost every day for an update. Sometimes she would know where he was, but other times she had no clue. He could have been anywhere. One day in April of 2007 I was in Mexico for a concert and I called her from my hotel room. The second she picked up the phone, I knew something was wrong. Fernando had jumped off the roof of a four-story building because he thought someone was chasing him. He'd shattered his leg in twelve places. He was in the hospital.

As soon as I got off the phone with his mother, I called him at the hospital and was able to get through to his room.

"I'm coming back," I told him.

"No, please. Do your concert and then come back. I'll still be here," he joked.

I performed that night and then flew back to LA and went straight to him. He was a mess. So thin and beat-up and a shadow of the man I'd known. But I could still see the spark of light in his eyes. I knew my Fernando was in there somewhere, and I vowed to stay by his side until he found himself. He stayed on the couch in his mother's house, and many nights I slept on the floor right next to him. I was seeing another guy at the time and he was so pissed at me. The guy and I broke up over it and I could not have cared less. My brother Pastor Pete and his wife, Ramona, would come over and pray for Fernando.

Slowly we started to see him coming back. Because he was immobile, he couldn't go anywhere to get a fix. Out of all of the things we had tried, the only remedy was his jumping off a four-story building.

We didn't officially get back together after that. We always stayed in touch, though, and we'd meet up for lunch or dinner. We'd meet up to talk, or not talk at all. Despite everything we had been through, I felt happy because I had my best friend back. I had gotten back the love and passion I had been missing for so long. But I was not going to be a fool either. I wanted to see if he was going to stay straight. I waited for him to get a steady job and a place of his own. I wanted the assurance that he was going to be okay. I could not go through that scenario all over again, and I could not put my kids through it either.

I knew that I would never love another man the way I loved Fernando. But I also knew that to truly love him, I had to love myself first. And to truly be there for him, I had to stand back and let him find his own way.

19

"Celibacy" and Sex Tapes

No tengo aires de la Salma
con la Machado nada que ver.
No tengo fama de la Trevi
estrella porno no quiero ser.

(*I do not have the airs of Salma*
I have nothing to do with Machado.
I do not have the fame of Trevi
I never wanted to be a porn star.)
—from "Dama Divina"

In October of 2007 my ex-husband Juan was arrested for drug trafficking and sentenced to ten years in prison. My two youngest children, Jenicka and Johnny, were devastated, and so was I. In the same year both the fathers of my children were put behind bars, and the man I loved was facing down the demons of a drug addiction. My father and brothers told me, "You are so good at everything else, but you are so shitty at picking men." I did not argue their point.

Throughout my heartbreak with Fernando I cried so much. "Why would God have me meet the love of my life and then not have me be able to be with him?" I used to ask Rosie.

To try to cheer me up she would say, "There is a man for you out there. Tell me what he is like."

So we started to make him up. "My husband wakes up at five in the morning and goes jogging. He takes care of himself. He eats healthy."

"And what do you call him?" Rosie asked.

"I call him Runner Boy."

Whenever I got down about Fernando, Rosie would say, "Tell me more about Runner Boy."

"Runner Boy is an older man. He is already successful. He doesn't need my money. He can buy me my engagement ring. And he is already retired. That way he has time for me."

"What does he look like?"

"He is tall and handsome. He knows how to dress and he always smells good."

"Is he a white man?"

"Oh, hell, no. I can't deal with pink balls. I want a sexy, romantic Mexican."

We were always dreaming about Runner Boy. When a man would approach me, Rosie and I used to turn to each other and say, "Oh, that's not Runner Boy." Or we would text it to each other from across the room: "Cute. But not Runner Boy." Or she would whisper in my ear as she passed, "You should F him. But he's not Runner Boy."

I should explain that Rosie stopped swearing and fucking around years before. To be exact, the date was Sunday, November 6, 2005. Rosie called me after church that day. Her voice was light and full of joy.

"Sister," she said to me, "something happened to me in church today. I feel only peace and love. I feel freed. God loves me and I love him and I'm going to live a different life."

"That's great, Sister. I am so happy!"

"And I'm not going to drink or do drugs or smoke."

"Good, Sister. This is all good."

"And I'm not going to have sex anymore."

I stayed quiet for a moment, trying to figure out how to respond nicely and truthfully to her.

"Sister, I love and support you, but you mean to tell me that you are going to be celibate?" I meant *abstinent*, but the concept was so alien to me that I didn't even know the right word.

After that, I would ask her all the time, "How is the abstinence going?"

In 2008 Rosie was dating a guy, and one day she called me, panicked. "I'm in trouble. I slipped up."

"Well, was it worth it?"

"Yeah, but it's still a sin! I'm afraid the whole church is going to find out. And I'm the pastor's sister!"

"How many people go to your church?" I asked.

"About four hundred."

"Okay, so you'll be embarrassed in front of about four hundred people? Let me make you feel better: I'm embarrassed in front of about four million."

"What do you mean?"

"I was giving this guy a blow job and he recorded it, and the video has been stolen. It's only a matter of time before it is going to show up on the Internet."

I was devastated. My brothers were going to see this. My father. My children. Could anything be more mortifying? That weekend I had a big concert and I asked Rosie and my mom to come with me. I needed their support.

That Friday night, Rosie and I were lying in my bed and I was still so pissed. I couldn't believe this little punk. He was one of my band members, and at the time he recorded the video, we were dating. I couldn't believe he would do this to me. He copied the video, and then it got passed down the line. Everybody in the *banda* world already knew about it, and in time the rest of the Latin music world would know as well.

"What do I do?" I asked Rosie.

"Just tell the truth. It's what couples do."

I decided that I would call my brothers and my dad and tell them about the video before they heard it from anyone else. Juan was ready to fuck up the guy, of course. Lupe was the first one to make me laugh about it.

"Don't be ashamed," he said. "It's good for a woman to suck a man's dick. We need more women like that. I'm sure you did a good job."

When I finished calling all of them, I turned to Rosie and said, "People are going to ask you about this. I want you to see it so you know what you are commenting on." I held the phone to her face.

"No!" she screamed. "I don't want to see that!"

"Watch it!" I insisted, holding the phone in her face. I wasn't backing down until she watched it. I waited as she stared at the phone for four minutes. When the video ended, I said, "Aren't I good at it? I should be a teacher. If I fail as a singer, I'll just be a porn star."

In June of that same year, 2008, I was arrested for assaulting a fan. I was onstage at my concert in Raleigh, North Carolina, when a man threw a full beer can onstage, nearly hitting me in the head, but it passed by me and hit one of my band members.

"Who threw that?" I said.

Three rows of fans pointed to one man.

"Get up here," I told him.

The man walked up to the stage and I popped him on the head

with my microphone. If it had been a normal microphone, it would just have left a bump. But this was a diamond-encrusted mic that my brother Juan had given me as a gift. It split the man's head open at the eyebrow, and he started to bleed. Security took him offstage and I didn't think much of it. You throw a beer can at me, you deserve what you get.

The Raleigh police did not agree. As soon as I finished the concert, they were waiting for me with handcuffs. They arrested me and held me on $50,000 bail. My brother Juan came to get me and posted the necessary $5,000. I got a lot of shit from the media for the incident. They said that I treated my fans horribly and I was a horrible person. I did feel bad about it, I will admit that. But if the situation played out again, I would probably do the same thing. I found out that the man's wife was a big fan of mine and he had gotten drunk that night. He claimed he didn't throw the beer can and that he only raised his hand because he thought he'd be able to dance with me. Which I guess you can say he did, in a way.

Again, people said I orchestrated the whole situation for the sake of media attention. Again, untrue. But I could see why people thought it was a publicity stunt. At the time, one of my hit singles was "Culpable o Inocente" (Guilty or Innocent). Since I got a pretty great mug shot out of that trip downtown, I decided to make T-shirts with a copy of my mug shot and the words "*Culpable o Inocente*" above the photo.

Fernando called me when he saw the mug-shot T-shirts. Though we were no longer dating, we never lost touch.

"Babe," he told me, "you are so ghetto."

"Shit. Thought I wasn't?"

20

Beso! Beso!

Yo soy una mujer de carne y hueso.
Yo soy una mujer que se enamora.

(*I am a woman of flesh and blood.*
I am a woman who falls in love.)
          —from "Yo Soy Una Mujer"

The man I'd popped with the microphone filed a lawsuit against me a few weeks after the concert in North Carolina. I guess that's a sure sign that you've made it. Nobody pressed charges against me when I was a nobody, but now that I had money in the bank, I had to pay for my stupid mistakes. I settled with him out of court, and I flew him and his entire family to sit in the front row of my upcoming concert on August 16, 2008, at the Nokia Theatre.

My goal when I started out was to make it to the Gibson Amphitheatre, where I had seen many of my idols perform. Of course, after I achieved that in 2006 and 2007, I came up with another goal: I wanted to make it to the Staples Center, which holds 20,000 fans. The Nokia, which holds 7,100, didn't exist when I was starting out. It had opened less than a year earlier, in October of 2007, and I considered it another stepping-stone on my way to the Staples. The concert was sold out that night, and for those three hours onstage I worked out all of my problems from the past year: Juan's going to prison, the trial with Trino, the drama with Fernando, my parents' ongoing divorce battle, the media backlash from my arrest, and the impending sex-tape bombshell. The tape still hadn't become public, but I knew it was only a matter of time. For those three hours onstage I was able to air out my private issues in such a public way, but only those who were closest to me knew all the details.

A little over three weeks later, on September 9, 2008, I released my tenth studio album (and fourteenth overall), *Jenni*. It was the first album I produced myself. I wanted to have control, but I also wanted to establish myself as more than just a recording artist. I know I am not going to be singing forever, so it was important to me that the industry and future artists knew that I can also produce. *Jenni* was my first album to hit number one on *Billboard*'s US Top Latin Albums chart.

Then, in the first days of October, while I was enjoying the success of that album, my fears came true. The sex tape was posted on the Internet by an anonymous source, and it spread like wildfire. Within hours I felt as if the entire world had seen it. The media attention was huge and immediate. Telemundo and Univision talked about it constantly.

Many people thought I myself had leaked the tape for publicity, which couldn't be further from the truth. That was the last kind of publicity I wanted. I was mortified and pissed beyond belief. And if I was going to intentionally leak a sex tape, I would have made sure the lighting was better. I was getting phone calls and e-mails asking if it was really me in the video and whether I wanted to talk about it. I didn't want to talk about it. I wanted to crawl into a cave and disappear, but I couldn't. That same month I found out I was nominated for a Latin Grammy for Best Ranchero Album for *La Diva en Vivo*. My fellow nominees were Vicente Fernández, Pepe Aguilar, Pedro Fernández, and Los Temerarios. I was so proud to have my name listed beside theirs. The producers of the Latin Grammys asked me to perform on the show on November 13 with my brother Lupe. It was the first time we sang together at such a prestigious event. I was proud to stand beside my brother on that stage with our whole family in the audience. I didn't win the Grammy that year, as suspected. When you are nominated in the same category as Vicente Fernández, you pretty much know what's going to happen.

Unfortunately, despite the Grammy nomination and the hit album, people were still more interested in the fucking sex tape. I decided to turn the embarrassment into something positive. I wrote "Dama Divina," which is an anthem for women to be proud of their bodies and their sexuality even if they do not look like a model or an actress. The guy in the video was twenty years younger than me. He was not Runner Boy. Not even close. When I crossed paths with him a few months later, I pounced on him and beat his ass. I bit him, busted his lip, and gave him a black eye before someone pulled me off him.

On December 7, 2008, I was scheduled to go back to Mazatlán, Mexico, to perform at a *palenque*. I was nervous because this was the city where the sex tape was filmed, and it was still all over the news there. I was nervous that the fans wouldn't accept me and would judge me for it. I decided I would address the issue as soon as I got onstage to get it out of the way.

"I was afraid to come to Mazatlán," I told the crowd. "Not because of what has been happening, but because one of the hardest parts of my life began here. That video that caused me so many tears."

The crowd started to cheer my name over and over. At that moment the embarrassment melted away. I felt so loved and so relieved.

Halfway through the concert my manager, Gabo, told me, "Esteban Loaiza is here and he wants to meet you." In Mazatlán and many parts of Mexico, Esteban Loaiza is an idol because he represented the country through baseball. He was a pitcher for more than twenty years in the big leagues, playing for several teams including the Chicago White Sox and the LA Dodgers. At the time, he was playing in Mexico. I invited him to come up on the stage. When he did, the fans started chanting, *"Beso! Beso!"*

For the sake of putting on a good show (and because he was handsome), I played along. "Can you believe it, *mijo*? These people want you to make me a baby," I told him.

He said with a smile, "Let's go." As he was walking off the stage, I grabbed his ass.

After the concert he came backstage to talk to me. By this point in my career, a lot of men were afraid to approach me, but Esteban was fearless. I also knew that he could get any girl he wanted in Mexico, and I wasn't about to kiss his feet. If he was interested, I was going to make him work a little.

He said, "Let me take you out to eat."

"I'm not hungry," I told him.

"A drink?"

"No, I'm not thirsty."

"Let me show you my town then."

"I've seen this town."

"Well, do you breathe? What about a walk for some air?"

I liked that he wasn't giving up, so I agreed. It was only the third after-party I had attended in my entire career. We went for a walk on the beach and then we went back to his house, where his buddies were all drinking. I had hurt my knee, so I took a painkiller and fell asleep in his room as he and his friends partied downstairs. I never even kissed the guy. The next night I caught my flight back home, but we kept in touch. We spoke every night until two or three in the morning. He never once mentioned the sex tape. He never mentioned the incident with the fan when I got arrested or any of the other media speculation about me. But I was sure he had heard of it, so I wanted to get it out in the open. So one day over the phone I decided to bring it up.

"You know what they say about me, right?" I asked him.

"Yes, but that is not who I see. I see the hardworking woman who fights for her kids."

The first time he came to pick me up at my house for a date, my children were all skeptical of him. They were skeptical of any man who tried to date me. He took me to dinner, and as we sat down at the restaurant, I got a text from my youngest son, Johnny, saying, "Do you know that Esteban has a criminal record?"

"What are you talking about?" I texted back.

Johnny wrote, "I googled him and it says he was arrested for a DUI in 2006. Are you sure you want to date this guy?"

I knew this was Johnny's way of telling me, "I'm looking out for you, Mom. I've got your back."

I showed Esteban the text. "Yes, it's true," he said, and explained that he'd had a few drinks after a game and he got stopped on the freeway for speeding. He said the experience changed him and he realized how stupid it was. We talked more about our careers and our backgrounds. We both came from humble beginnings and were close to our families. It was your typical first date "getting to know you" conversation.

When I got home, Chiquis and Jacqie were waiting up to hear how it went.

"So?" Chiquis asked. "Tell me everything."

"He was nice," I replied. "It was nice."

"But you're not that into him?" she asked.

"I didn't say that."

Jacqie, who is not one to hide her true feelings, said, "You know, Mom, he seems like a cock."

While it is true that I didn't fall head over heels for him right away, he was sweet, handsome, and easy to be around. Soon enough that combination won me over. I realized that everything about this love was different from the love I had with Fernando. It's true, there wasn't the same passion and fire. But there were also no raging fights, no phone calls at four in the morning, no dramas. I told my family, "Fernie was a passionate love. But this is a mature love." And a mature love is what I needed at that point in my life. Esteban and I understood each other in a lot of ways. He had his own fame and understood the good, the bad, and the constant demands that come with it. I was still in touch with Fernando here and there, and I would get updates on him through his mother. Though I still cared for him, I knew that he would never be able to provide me the stability that Esteban could.

My family grew to love and appreciate Esteban for the way he treated me. He took care of my every need. He was always asking, "Are you hungry? Do you need anything? What can I do for you?" He was the man I had dreamed of—this was Runner Boy. He had his own money. He'd had a successful career. He took care of himself. And he treated me like a queen and my kids like princes and princesses.

In January of 2009 the news of our relationship went public. That same month I bought a home in Encino, California. I was tired of driving from Corona to LA all the time. I needed to be closer to where the action was, but I couldn't bring myself to sell my home in Corona. It wasn't smart financially, but I held on to it and continued to pay the bills though nobody was living in it. That was my first dream home. For me it represented so much. It represented that I was making good on my promises to my children, that I was proving Trino wrong, and that a poor little Mexican girl from Long Beach who once lived in a back garage could rise up and buy a seven-thousand-square-foot home.

This new home was even bigger at almost ten thousand square feet, with views of Los Angeles and the valley as far as the eye could see. I remember walking through that house the first night and asking myself, "How can it be that I once couldn't pay the water bill on my little two-bedroom in Compton, and now I own a home with eleven bathrooms?" Not only that, I had finally found a man who treated me right, who wasn't jealous or possessive, who had his own money and didn't need anything from me but love and loyalty. And that's all I needed back from him. Though we had only been together a few months, I had never felt so secure in my personal life.

And then, in May of that same year, Esteban and I broke up.

I caught him in a white lie and I ended it right then and there. For the few months that we had been together, he had done this multiple times, and it pissed me off. He would lie about the stupidest shit. I would always call him on it, but he continued to do it. I'd had enough of being lied to by men, and I wasn't going to go through it again.

That same month my brother Juan was in the final rounds of a singing-contest show in Mexico called *El Gran Desafío de Estrellas*. He asked me to sing a song with him on one of the shows, and of course I said yes. I could never say no to Juan. The show taped every Sunday in Mexico City. That weekend I had shows in the cities of Hermosillo and Obregón and in Jalisco. After my last performance on Saturday night I flew to Mexico City to sing with my brother the following day. The show was broadcast on Azteca, the second-biggest network in

Mexico. The biggest network, Televisa, sent me an e-mail saying that if I went on *El Gran Desafío de Estrellas*, they would ban me from their network.

When I told Juan, he said, "Don't worry about it. It's not worth it."

I said, "You're my brother and I don't give a fuck."

Less than fifteen minutes after we sang, I received an e-mail saying that I was officially banned from Televisa.

The next morning I went to the Mexico City airport to fly back to LA. I had the cash on me from the concert on Saturday night— a little over $50,000. When they searched my bag and found it, they asked me why I didn't declare it.

"I'm sorry, I didn't know I had to," I explained. "Let me do it now."

"You can't," they told me before they arrested and detained me.

I had to pay an $8,000 fine and then they released me. By the time I made it to LA, the news was everywhere. The first network to cover it, of course, was Televisa, despite their having said they would never report any news on me ever again. By this point in my career I understood how the media played the game, and I wasn't going to be a part of it as long as I could help it.

Around that same time, Graciela Beltrán, during an appearance on *El Gordo y la Flaca*, said how I was always jealous of her because she was the pretty one. Most artists knew that when someone said something like that about me, I wasn't going to back down and then they'd be able to say, "There goes Jenni Rivera fighting again." But this time it was different. When Graciela started talking shit about me, it clicked: they were using me to get publicity and ratings. So I refused to respond.

Six months later Graciela said something again. I was so tired of the bitch, but I refused to give her publicity by fighting with her in the media. Instead, I wrote a song called "Ovarios." I talked shit about her in the song lyrics instead of on any show. "Yeah, you may be the queen," I sang, "but it's in an abandoned town." It took me many years to figure out what the rappers had taught me way back in my high school days: the best way to settle your shit is through a song. That way you win the feud and you get the royalties.

21

Letting Go

Cómo sufrió por ella
que hasta en su muerte la fue llamando.

(*How he suffered for her*
and even when he was dying, he was calling to her.)
—from "Cucurrucucu Paloma"

On July 1, 2009, my sister and I were going to celebrate our
birthdays together as we did every year. Except this time it would
be on a three-story yacht in Long Beach. We had planned for a DJ
and Los Herederos de Nuevo León to play that night. A few hundred
people were invited. The press wanted to cover the event. Everything
had been set since the beginning of June. We were all looking forward to it, but I put all plans on hold when we were informed that
my ex-husband Juan had fallen ill in his cell at California City Correctional Center, where he was serving the second year of his ten-
year sentence for drug trafficking. He was transferred to Lancaster's
Antelope Valley Hospital. I had expected him to get better, but as the

days dragged on, it didn't seem as if it was going to happen. He had pneumonia and was suffering from complications due to an infection. I opted to cancel the big party and have a small dinner instead. My sister and I invited a few friends to my home in Encino for a quiet birthday celebration. I was too worried about Juan's condition to even think about celebrating my birthday. Juan was the father of my two youngest children, and they were both so close to him. I couldn't stand the thought of Johnny and Jenicka losing their father at seven and eleven years old. And though Juan and I battled from 2003 to 2007 over our divorce, we had long since put that behind us and became good friends once again. When he was incarcerated in 2007, I made a point to take my children to see him often, and sometimes I would even go alone. Juan and I could always talk through our shit with each other, and as we grew close once more, I considered him one of my best friends.

The morning of July 1, I got a call telling me that things had taken a turn for the worse. I went to visit Juan, and as I walked into his room I saw his sister Erika sitting there with a pale face. Immediately I knew something was terribly wrong. I turned to see Juan lying in the bed, his hands cuffed to the metal bars. His eyes were open halfway. His body was shaking left and right. It seemed as if the medical instrument he had going through his mouth, down his throat, and into his lung was pumping oxygen so heavily it made his entire body shudder. His arms and legs moved from side to side as his chest pumped up and down. The look in his half-open eyes told me so much. Yes, he was in a coma, but for some reason his eyes had opened due to the swelling in his face. It was a terrible sight.

"What's wrong with him!" I suddenly screamed. "What happened?"

"I don't know," said his sister. "The nurses aren't telling me anything."

"What do you mean, they're not telling you anything? Where the fuck are they?"

A nurse stormed in as she heard me screaming out of control. I had to be quiet or I was going to be asked to leave, she said. She walked me out of the room and into the hallway, where I had left Johnny and Jenicka.

"What's wrong, Mommy?" they asked. "What happened to Daddy?"

I hadn't been this upset on any of the other days we had visited, but I just couldn't hold it in this time. How the fuck was I going to tell my babies that their father might not make it? They were so close to him. Even after he went to jail, I would bring them to him and they maintained a beautiful bond. I put my face against the hallway window, not wanting my kids to see me cry.

I grabbed my BlackBerry from my purse and dialed Chiquis's number.

"Mama, what's wrong?" she asked as soon as she heard me crying. "Why are you crying like this? How's Dad?"

I told her he was very sick and that I knew he didn't want me to leave. I told her how he looked and asked her to come and pick the kids up at the hospital. I also asked her to cancel the dinner party and to let our guests know that I was going to spend the rest of the day at the hospital with Juan. That night at midnight my hairstylist, Ivan, and his boyfriend, Rafa, came to visit me as I sat with Juan in the hospital. Elena, my jeweler, and her girlfriend, Zuleyma, showed up as well. Though I had broken up with Esteban two months earlier, he drove all the way from San Diego to be there. They brought cake and mole and sang "Happy Birthday" to me.

The next day, on my actual birthday, it was just my seven-year-old son, Johnny, and me sitting next to Juan in room 233 of the intensive care unit at Lancaster's Antelope Valley Hospital. He wanted to be with his dad. "Thank you for spending your birthday here with my daddy," Johnny said to me. "You're a good mommy." Johnny cried so much that day. He held his father's hand and prayed, "Please, God, save my daddy. Let him live. I promise to be a good boy. I won't say bad words anymore. I'll do my homework and share my PlayStation with my sister. I'll pray every night. I'll do my chores. God, please let my daddy live." It broke my heart in a million pieces and I felt so powerless.

I had been through so much with Juan. Now this. Could it be that I was going to have to take our kids to their father's funeral? No. I couldn't live through that.

At 11:00 p.m. I was still getting birthday texts and phone calls. Johnny was asleep in a chair in the corner. Earlier that day the nurse told me Juan only had a 40 percent chance of living. As I watched Johnny sleep, I tried to come to terms with having to step in and be his father as well as his mother. Neither of my sons would grow up with his father, and I had to fill that role. It scared the shit out of me. To comfort Juan, I sang his favorite songs, and at the sound of my voice, tears rolled down his face. In this way, I said my last good-byes to the father of my children, my ex-husband, and my great friend.

On July 14, 2009, Juan died in his hospital bed in Lancaster, California. He was all alone. The hospital was mobbed by the press. I was not allowed to go see him. Neither were Johnny or Jenicka, his sisters, his parents, or his girlfriend. I knew it was my fault. He had married and had kids with a celebrity, and for that he had to pay the unfair price of being alone on his last day on earth.

Before Juan passed, I asked him what he wanted his funeral to be like. He told me he wanted his favorite singer, Coyote, to be there, so I made sure it happened. In my mind it was the only way I could make it up to Juan, because I felt such guilt that he crossed over without anyone by his side.

My whole family attended his funeral as though he were still my husband and he were still their brother. Juan had been a handsome man. But by the time he passed, after so many days spent at the hospital, he was so swollen. He looked many pounds heavier.

"This is not Juan," I told Chiquis as we knelt in front of his open casket. "He wouldn't be happy with the way he looks. When I die, I want a closed casket. Promise me, princess. Make sure it's a closed casket if something happens to me."

Juan's passing changed me in so many ways. It gave me a perspective on what was important. By this point in my career I was selling out every concert, and all my albums were going gold and platinum. I was dominating the regional music industry, and I had achieved all I had dreamed of and even more. Yet all I wanted was to be home with my kids. I decided that I was not going to miss another birthday, Mother's Day, Father's Day, Thanksgiving, Christmas, or New Year's Day. It didn't matter how lucrative the opportunity was or how prestigious. I was going to be with my family.

Shortly after Juan died, I got back together with Esteban. I was willing to forgive him for lying to me, but I told him that there could be no more secrets between us, no matter how small. He agreed to the deal and treated me even better than before. He took care of my every need and showered me with gifts.

Once he came home with three Louis Vuitton purses for no reason. My closet started to overflow with the designer shoes and high-end clothes he loved to buy for me. "Babe," I told him, "thank you, but I don't need all this." He didn't listen. He wasn't just generous with me, he was the same way with my kids and my family. Whatever anyone wanted, Esteban would provide. Every day he walked in the door with more and more bags. Though I begged him not to get me anything else, it did feel good to have a man who could spoil me so horribly. I mean, I wasn't going to say no to another Louis Vuitton bag. (But, really, who needs fourteen fucking pairs of sneakers?)

On July 29, my family and I had an interview with Piolín on the radio station La Nueva. Some family members were in the studio with me and some were on the phone. Piolín was asking my mom and dad, "So when is your daughter getting married to Esteban?"

"Whenever she wants," Dad responded.

"So you'd be okay if she married this guy?"

"If she wants," my mother said.

Then Esteban called in to say hello, and Piolín asked him straight out, "When are you going to propose? We asked her parents and they said it was okay."

Esteban said, "Really, you'd approve if I asked?"

"If you love her, go for it," both my parents said.

My dad added, "But you shouldn't sleep with a man before you are married."

A little late on that advice, don't you think?

About a month before Juan's death, Jacqie, who was then nineteen, came to me and told me she was pregnant. The first words out of my mouth were to tell her that she didn't have to move out. I had promised myself that if one of my daughters told me she was pregnant, I would not make the same mistake that my parents and so many parents of their generation made. "He can move into this house if he wants," I said. "But you should stay here with that baby."

On November 17, 2009, Jacqie went into labor. I coached her through every step of the way, telling her, "You don't need an epidural. You can do this shit on your own." And she did. A few hours later I met my first grandchild, Jaylah Hope, and I knew right then that my life would never again be the same. Nothing made me prouder than being a mother. Nothing made me softer than being a grandmother. Jaylah changed my world in so many ways; one of the biggest was that she strengthened my relationship with Jacqie. Jacqie is my rebel child, the one who cannot be tamed or told no. Just like her mama. Because of this we clashed a lot during her teenage years, but when Jaylah came along, Jacqie and I grew so close. She is still my rebel child and will always be. I hope that Jaylah turns out to be just like both of us so Jacqie can know how wonderful and frustrating it is to have a daughter who cannot be told no.

22

The Fairy Tale and the Reality Show

Well, they're flickin' on the bar lights
Band's playin' one last song.

—from "You Don't Have to Go Home"

A few months after the interview with Piolín, someone in my family heard that Esteban was shopping for a ring. When one Rivera hears something, every Rivera hears it.

Rosie approached him and asked him straight out, "You're going to ask my sister to marry you, aren't you?"

"Maybe," he told her.

"Are you asking her because you love her or because you feel pressure from the media? Don't do it because of that."

"I'm asking her because I love her."

On January 21, 2010, Esteban took me and my five kids out for sushi. Halfway through dinner he pretended something fell on the floor, and he went to pick it up. When he got back up, he had a ring in

199

his hand. "I love you," he told me. "I love your kids and your family. I want to spend the rest of my life with you. Will you marry me?"

I was in shock and didn't speak at first.

"Answer him, Mom!" my kids yelled at me.

Once I said yes, he put this incredible ten-carat ring on my finger. He said, "I brought the kids because I know I am not just marrying you, I am marrying them too."

I called my sister, my brothers, my mom, and my dad to give them the news (though I'm sure they all saw it coming before I did). I was so happy and so excited. I had never been proposed to before. And I certainly hadn't received a ring like that before.

A month later when we were planning our wedding, I called Rosie to ask her to be my maid of honor.

"Really?" she said. "You want me? With all of your famous friends, you pick me?"

"Well, yeah. Who the fuck else would I pick?"

Around that time Esteban's mom told me, "You are taking a good man." It felt as if she were punching me in the gut and telling me that I was not good enough for her son.

"Yes," I said, "he is a good guy. And I'm a good woman."

The conversation bothered me for a few days, but then I forgot about it until one day, as we got closer to the wedding, Esteban asked me for a prenup. I was completely thrown off. I'd never once asked him how much he made or how much he had in the bank. I never asked to look at his finances. I didn't care. I had my own money.

That's when I remembered my conversation with his mother and I understood the prenup was her idea: she thought I wanted him for his money.

So I went back to Manley Freid, the same attorney who had helped me settle my divorce with Juan and helped my mother in her divorce from my dad. I told Manley I needed a prenup. Manley and Esteban's attorney worked on that prenup until the day before the wedding.

Something about the prenup pissed me right the fuck off and made me nostalgic for the relationship I had had with Fernando. Sure we fought, but we had passion and fire and we trusted in our love. And we didn't make each other sign any fucking legal document to prove it.

I called Fernando up and demanded, "Are you ever going to get your shit together? Because if you don't, I'm going to marry this guy."

"So marry him."

"I'm serious. I'll do it."

"Go ahead. Do it. What do I care?"

Esteban and I were married on September 8, 2010, at Hummingbird Nest Ranch, in Simi Valley. Everything about the wedding was gorgeous and perfect. And decadent. I flew in aboard a helicopter wearing a custom-made Eduardo Lucero dress. We had eight hundred guests and a ton of security so that nobody had to worry about getting his or her picture taken. Every detail was thought out and taken care of. During her maid-of-honor speech Rosie said, "You met Runner Boy, Sister. He really exists."

I cried throughout the whole ceremony and reception. Part of me was crying with happiness because I was finally getting the fairy-tale wedding I'd always wanted. And part of me was crying with sadness because I worried that I was making a mistake.

That's not to say our marriage wasn't beautiful. It was, for some time. He traveled with me everywhere, he took care of me and my kids. He calmly entered into my world of craziness, which had grown a bit more crazy that year, since I had just agreed to do my reality show, *I Love Jenni*, with the mun2 network.

When I got into watching a lot of the reality shows around 2007, I said to myself, "Well, fuck, my life is better than a *novela*. I should have one of those." I wanted the world to see what really went on in my life. The media misconstrued things or flat-out made them up or exaggerated the facts. I wanted people to see that I was a girl from the hood who had made good. I knew it would be entertaining, but I also wanted it to inspire. I tried to sell it to a few of the big networks, but none of them wanted it.

"Fuck them," I said, "we'll do it on our own." I made a pilot episode and mun2, Telemundo's English-language sister network, wanted to take it. But by then I had become so busy with all my other projects that I didn't think I even had the time for it. I suggested that they do a show based on Chiquis, and I would be the executive producer and appear on it when I could.

I knew Chiquis had the personality for it. She is funny, smart, sassy, and she is surrounded by a bunch of crazy-ass characters (one of them being her mama). We came up with the idea for a show called *Jenni Rivera Presents: Chiquis & Rac-Q*. Rac-Q was one of her friends, but she quit in the middle of it and then Chiquis carried the show.

After that first season I realized that it would be a great opportunity for all of the kids if I also did a show focused on me, so I decided I would make the time for it. That's when I came up with *I Love Jenni*. After the success of Chiquis's show, every single network that had rejected my pitch now wanted to do a show with me. But I wouldn't consider leaving mun2. I have always said that I will stick with the people who believed in me first.

I saw *I Love Jenni* as a way to make money for my kids and show them how to work. And make no mistake, filming a reality show is hard work. A lot of days it's a huge pain in the ass. At times I wanted to hide from the cameras, but it was not an option. The production team shows up on your front step that morning ready to work, and we all have to show up too, no matter how shitty the day was going.

In December of 2010, we went through one of those shitty days, when my son Michael was accused of rape. He was nineteen and he had slept with a minor. When they broke up, the girl told her mother that she had had sex with Mikey.

I sat down with Mikey and asked him what had happened. I couldn't believe that he would mistreat a female. He had grown up surrounded by women, and I never once saw him be anything but kind and tender. Mikey told me he had slept with this girl, but it had been consensual. It was decided to defend the allegations in court.

Before the case began, Rosie presented me the Victory Ring that I had given her during the trial with Trino. "This is for you," she said. "Justice will be done again." The case came to a close in March of 2011 when Mikey was given three years' probation and a $600 fine.

Just when the saga with Mikey ended, a new one began with my longtime manager Gabo. I had a concert in Mexico where we were paid in cash. One of Gabo's assistants borrowed a leather bag from the head security guard so he wouldn't be carrying around the funds in his hands. When the assistant returned the bag to the security guard at the end of the night, the original contract was in the bag.

I looked at the contract and didn't recognize any of the numbers. The tickets sold were more than I had been told; the amount I was paid was double what Gabo told me I was getting paid. For years, family and friends had been telling me that Gabo was not trustworthy, and now here it was in black and white on a legal document. It appeared as if he was taking half of my proceeds from the concert in addition to his management fee. We looked into the contracts, and it seemed that at every appearance where I was making $200,000,

I would receive only $100,000. We estimated that the total amount owed to me was between $1 million and $2.5 million.

Gabo knew more than anyone else how hard I worked. He knew how tiring and demanding it was to constantly be on the go, yet I always showed up and gave 100 percent. He knew how painful it was for me to be away from my kids. He also knew that everything I did, I did for them. I worked so hard to provide them with everything I never had. In my mind, Gabo did not hurt me. He did something for worse. The son of a bitch hurt my children.

The following week Gabo and I were in Acapulco chilling by the pool and eating lunch. At a quiet, calm moment I presented the issue.

"I know what you did," I told Gabo. "There have been discrepancies in the payments and you owe me money."

He denied it, and that made me even angrier. Here's the thing: If I catch people doing something and they admit to it, I can forgive them right away. If they deny it, game on. Gabo and I had been together for over ten years. After all that time, you'd think he'd know who he was fucking with.

I left him in Acapulco and did not care how he made his way home.

I cried for Gabo as if it were a breakup. It wasn't about the money. People had lied to me before, but they were never people I considered family. And that's how I felt about Gabo. He was a brother who had betrayed me for so long when I was so loyal to him in return.

On May 20, 2011, I performed at La Feria de Guanajuato, in Guanajuato, Mexico. During the show a fan threw a full beer can onstage that skimmed my head and landed in the center of the *palenque*. My brother Juan was standing on the sidelines and went nuts. When it comes to his family, Juan loses all sense of control. He went after the guy and beat him up pretty bad. Two weeks later a video surfaced, and the media frenzy began. Juan received a thousand death threats. Two weeks before this incident a female fan threw a beer can at me and I brought her onstage and poured a beer over her head. I got crucified for that as well. I am not saying that I was right, but when you have a full beer can flying at you onstage, you kind of lose your head.

People said the Riveras were killers and that we would go to Mexico to fill our pockets with money and humiliate the fans. I was scared. I thought I was going to lose my fan base. We held a press conference on June 7 and I apologized to my fans and reassured them about how important they were to me. I admitted my mistakes and took all the heat. I knew Juan had made a mistake, but he was my baby brother, my Angel Face, and I was going to stand by him.

The following week, on June 16 and 17, I had two back-to-back concerts at the prestigious Auditorio Nacional in Mexico City. I was afraid that nobody would show up. Once again, despite all of my imperfections, all of my flaws, the fans were there for me. Both nights were sold out. My fans held me up when I was so down on myself. They supported me when I was judging myself so harshly. They gave me love that I did not deserve.

On July 29, 2011, I had a concert date in Reynosa, Mexico, a town notorious for its drug cartels. A few days before I was set to perform, I got a phone call from the FBI telling me not to go sing.

"Why not?" I asked.

"Because we got an informant inside a cartel, and they are planning to kidnap you."

I thought it was bullshit. Anybody could call me from the FBI and tell me that. The FBI agent gave me a number and I called it. An FBI agent in San Diego answered. Oh, shit, I thought. This is real. I called my brother Juan to see if he could get some of his buddies in Mexico to protect me.

He called me back a half hour later: "I spoke to the main guy there. Nothing is going to happen."

We were all still nervous. My band was already in Mexico waiting for me to arrive. The band told the promoters that they weren't going to do the concert, so in retaliation the promoters held two of my employees hostage, demanding that I perform.

That night a hurricane came through Texas and hit the town in Mexico where I was going to land. It was the perfect excuse to bail out, but then at 7:00 p.m. the airport reopened. Juan drove to my house and begged me not to go.

"I have to," I said. "If I don't go, they will come after me or you or Lupe in the future. We can't show fear."

Months earlier, when there had been another scare during one of my concerts in Mexico, the fans had started to leave. So I said to them, "I get paid to sing, not run. Stay here with me." I felt the same way now. I was not going to run. I was not going to be intimidated.

"If you go, then I'm going with you," Juan said.

"No. You stay here."

"No, Chay, I'm going."

"I'm not asking you, Juan. I'm telling you. If something happens to me, you're the only one who can take care of things. I'm going to take Esteban. You know where the money is. And, Brother, if anything happens to me, I want a red casket with butterflies."

I flew from Van Nuys to McAllen with my team, among them my assistant Julie, my makeup artist Jacob, and my second assistant Vaquero. We played music the entire flight, specific songs that I had chosen. We were pressed for time, so I had to get ready on the plane. Jacob got to work on my makeup and Julie started on my hair. We listened to "Cuando Muere Una Dama" over and over again. As we walked off the plane Jacob, Julie, and I cried. Vaquero just stared in shock. I told Jacob and Vaquero they could stay at hotel and wait until we got back. I didn't even give Julie that option. I knew she wouldn't leave me.

We got in a car that was surrounded by the fourteen Hummers and they drove us from the border to the venue. I had never felt such heat or tension. When we arrived, the building was surrounded by even more Hummers, but there were also military tanks and soldiers at every door and undercover among the crowd. We had the protection of the government, the military, and the cops, both good and bad.

I put it out of my mind as I sang for hours and drank the tequila shots my fans offered me, just as I did at every one of my performances. That day I may have had even more tequila than usual. After I stepped offstage, I was escorted right back to the Hummers, where the marines were waiting. We headed back to the border the same way we had come, surrounded by a caravan of marines and nervous as fuck. Once we crossed back over into Texas, we all could finally breath normally again. But I felt as if I had to get out of this life. I couldn't live this way any longer. Of course I didn't know how to pull myself out of it.

On July 26, 2011, I was presented with a star at the Poly Walk of Fame Ceremony at Long Beach Poly. Since I started recording music in 1993 I have been given many awards. I have appreciated every one, but to receive this recognition from the place where it all began was incredibly special. I have always been so proud to be from Long Beach and that I attended "the home of scholars and champions," even though I attended for only a few months because I got pregnant. When I left Poly at fifteen years old I was so upset. To be asked back twenty-seven years later and recognized for my achievements was the ultimate honor.

On September 3, 2011, I made it to the Staples Center, the end goal in the LA music scene. The place where I said that once I got there, I would retire. I was the first female regional Mexican artist to ever perform there. The funny thing was, I had worked so hard to get to that stage and dreamed of how great it would be, and then it really wasn't. It was too big. It didn't have the intimacy of the Gibson or the Kodak. I felt the same when I played at the Auditorio Nacional in Mexico City. Though I could make a lot more money playing at venues such as the Staples Center or the Auditorio Nacional, I preferred to play at smaller theaters and *palenques*. The following year I did two back-to-back gigs at the Gibson instead of the large concert at the Staples.

In October of 2011 I launched a radio show called *Contacto Directo con Jenni Rivera*. I was tired of being a media pawn and hearing all the lies and rumors about me. I saw the show as an opportunity for me to make statements or announcements directly to my fans, but also to have conversations with them. To talk about real issues with them and offer them help or advice from my experiences.

I asked Rosie to be on it with me, but she was skeptical at first because she thought she was boring and would have nothing to talk about, but I eventually talked her into it. All we had to do was be ourselves. The way we talked to each other was how we talked on the radio. We did it live from a studio for four hours every Wednesday. The executives told me not to talk about two things: politics and religion. So I talked freely about both. These topics affect my people, and I wasn't going to be influenced or scared. I kept it real for my fans, and they thanked me by tuning in week after week.

We started in thirteen markets. Within a few months we were in forty markets, and by the end of the year in fifty-seven. I was convinced now more than ever that I wanted to have my own talk show.

Though I told myself I would slow down in 2012, I was busier than ever. Not only did I have concerts every weekend, I had the reality show, the radio show, a boutique I was planning, and a taco truck I was launching. I was also taking acting lessons, and I was a judge for *La Voz . . . México*. Esteban came with me wherever I went. While a part of me liked having a companion by my side and I appreciated that he took care of me, I also felt suffocated at times. I would tell him I needed my space, and he would get bored and go shopping for me. He would come home with his car full of bags, and everyone in the family would go out to help him cart the bags inside. I realized that maybe he had a problem, but if it made him happy and kept him out of my hair, what the fuck did I care what he did with his money?

By the time the summer came around, I had a thousand things going on at once, but at the forefront of my mind was that Mikey's girlfriend, Drea, was about to have a baby, my second grandchild. On August 26, 2012, I flew down to Mexico for a few days to tape *La Voz*. I told Drea, "Don't have this baby until I get back." But the baby had other plans. As I was sitting in my judge chair on August 28, I kept checking my phone for news. During a break a text came through: a photo of my second gorgeous granddaughter, Luna Amira. I was upset that I was not there to welcome her into the world, but so excited to get home to meet another princess I could spoil and teach the big-booty song.

23

Butterfly of the Hood

Ya me canso de llorar y no amanece
Ya no sé si maldecirte o por tí rezar.

(*I'm tired of crying with no hope*
I don't know whether to curse you or pray for you.)
—from "Paloma Negra"

In 2011 I got a call from the Hispanic Godfather of Hollywood, Edward James Olmos. "I need a big favor from you," he said. "I need you to work with me on a film. I'll send you the script and you tell me if you like it."

He explained that he wanted me to play the role of Maria, a drug-addicted mother who is in prison. The movie is called *Filly Brown*, and it tells the story of a Latina rapper who struggles to make it in the game. I didn't need to read the script to say yes. The fact that Edward James Olmos saw something in me that I didn't see in myself was enough of a reason for me to sign on.

As with everything I do, I wasn't going to half-ass it. I was going to do it to the best of my ability. I trained with an acting coach and I rehearsed with my costars for the entire month leading up to the filming. I was surrounded by such amazing and generous talent. I loved being on that set. There was a special atmosphere and camaraderie among the actors and crew, who, by the way, were being paid so little for this tiny independent film. I was getting a thousand dollars.

During breaks on set I talked to the crew and cameramen. There was one still photographer who I talked to for a while and I found out that he was not being paid at all. He needed the money way more than I did, so I asked the production to give my check to him.

I wasn't in it for the money—I said from the beginning I would do it for free, and I was true to my word. I wasn't in it for the glamour—my character was stripped down, no makeup, and drugged out half the time. I was in it because Edward James Olmos had asked me, because I loved the story, and because I wanted to prove to myself that I could. Most of all I wanted my kids to be proud of me. I wanted them to be able to look on the big screen one day and say, "That's my mom. Isn't she cool?"

I never even considered acting before, but I never seriously considered singing when I started out and look where that got me. A few months after the movie was finished, the acting world came calling once more.

In September of 2012 my manager had set up meetings with huge entertainment executives at Fox, CBS, NBC, and ABC. They were interested in doing a sitcom loosely based on my life and starring me. I couldn't believe that any of these execs even wanted to meet with me. I didn't want to get ahead of myself, but I thought this might be my way out of performing and traveling so much. I would finally be able to stay home with the kids on the weekends.

I felt that something was shifting in my life for the better. Not only did I have the meetings set up with the TV execs, but there were also talks of my getting a residency, a regular gig for a certain amount of time under contract, in Vegas. I figured that I could do the sitcom, the residency, and then maybe travel once or twice a month for concerts in Mexico. It would allow me more time to be home with my kids, which is all I wanted.

Jacqie got married on September 19, 2012, one of the happiest days of my life. I got to walk her down the aisle, and I remember feeling truly at peace. I had my five incredible children around me, my two beautiful granddaughters, and a supportive man beside me. I thought I couldn't ask for anything more.

On September 21, that all went to shit. Esteban told a lie about someone he had called, and when I confronted him about it, he denied it. Two days later I brought it up again. "Just tell me the truth," I told him "I already know it, so just admit it." But he still denied it. I was so pissed and I told him to get out of the house for a few days so I could cool off. He packed a bag and headed to his mother's in San Diego. I told him I would call him when I was ready to talk. As I watched him walk away, I felt something in my gut. Something was not right.

The following day I discovered evidence of even more lies and deception. I was done. I had warned him so many times that I could not stand liars and I would not put up with lying. I do not go back on my word.

Esteban kept calling and texting to come back home. "I need more time," I told him. "Give me a few more days."

On October 1 I found myself sitting in Manley Freid's office once again. Rosie came with me.

"You are making me a lot of money, young lady. I can live just off of you," he told me. "The next time you think of dating someone, bring him to me. Not your mom, not your dad, me. I can see you are amazing at everything you do except choosing men." Then he asked Rosie, "Isn't she bad at choosing men? Tell her the truth."

Rosie turned to me and said, "We are bad at choosing men."

Manley said, "I wasn't asking about you. Tell her *she* is bad at it."

Of course Rosie didn't have it in her to be that harsh.

I got sad when we started to divide whatever wasn't protected. The good news is that a lot of it was protected, thanks to the amazing prenup.

"Manley," I said, "would I get in trouble if I took all of his clothes and burned them in my backyard? What if I get one of those big trash bins and put them in there and then burn them?"

"No, don't do it. His attorney will make you compensate him for every piece of clothing."

"Ah, fuck," I said. "Well, it was a beautiful wedding, wasn't it?"

"It was a beautiful wedding," Rosie assured me.

"A beautiful mistake. I should never have married a man I didn't love passionately. One day I'll put the dress up in a museum with a plaque that says WORN ONCE, BY MISTAKE."

This would be my third divorce. I wanted to deliver the papers myself, but obviously I knew that a third party had to do it. I made a plan with Pete Salgado, my business manager, for him to deliver the papers, but not before I had a chance to say my last piece to Esteban.

I told Esteban that I would meet him at his mother's house in San Diego because I had our wedding album for her. It had finally been delivered, and I wanted to give it to his mom myself. When I got to her house, Esteban wasn't there yet. I sat with his mother, going through the pictures and talking about what a beautiful day it had been. Soon Esteban walked in and I greeted him by saying, "Hey, is there anything you want to tell me?"

"No. Why?"

I told him that I knew everything he had done. I told his family the whole truth, including details that are too horrible to admit in writing. His family got upset, calling me all sorts of names and telling me that I was a liar. I had said all I needed to say. I stood up and walked out the front door as they continued to hurl insults at my back. As I walked out, Pete walked in and delivered the papers to Esteban.

As I drove away from Esteban and back to my home and children, my own lyrics played back to me. I realized that I hadn't just written these songs for other women. I wrote them for me too. I started writing songs because I wanted the world to know that it was good to be a woman and it was okay not to have the perfect little life. It was okay to be beautiful in your own way, to be strong, get an education, pursue your own career. It wasn't shameful to be a single mother. There is pride in getting up every morning, pulling your kids through, and living for them. I wanted to make that all acceptable. I wanted women everywhere to be able to say, "Hey, I can do this."

I can do this, I repeated to myself. But inside I was still crumbling. Something about this divorce was different from the others. Maybe it was because I thought I was older and wiser and I wouldn't let this kind of shit happen to me anymore. Or maybe it was because Esteban had pretended to be one man and was another man entirely. Over the next few weeks I found out he had betrayed my trust in so many ways.

I just wanted my mother. I drove to her neighborhood and circled her house, but I could not find the courage to go inside. I was so afraid of her seeing me in so much pain. I called Rosie to tell her where I was. Rosie was living with Mom, and I thought that if there were any two people I wanted to be with at that moment, it was them. But I also was afraid of showing them my weak side. I had always been the strong one, and now I felt so helpless.

"Come in," Rosie said.

"I don't want you to see me like this. Don't lose respect for me. I think this is what is going to break me."

"Never. Nothing will break you. Come here, please."

"I don't want Mom to see me cry. I'm afraid if I fall in her arms I will never stop crying."

"Don't be scared for Mom. She is strong. She can handle it."

As I turned the corner once more and headed for my mother's driveway, I saw one of her friends pull up. I drove past the house and back onto the freeway.

The following day I got a call from Pete Salgado telling me that not one but all four networks wanted my sitcom. Ten years earlier when I was driving around dropping off my demo tapes and having doors slammed in my face, I said that one day people were going to believe in the little Mexican girl from the LBC. As I climbed the ladder of my career step by step, I saw that come true. But I never imagined that four of the mainstream networks would offer me the chance to be the first Mexican woman to star in my own sitcom. This was it. This was my exit route. As I told my family, I was still in shock. I said with tears in my eyes, "They love me. They really love me."

Three days later I had one of the most beautiful and joyful days of my life on October 6, when I threw Jenicka her quinceañera. I got to give her the quinceañera I never had, with three hundred people at a beautiful hall in Montebello. Jenicka is the one child who has never made me cry. She is this incredibly bright, sweet, beautiful person, and you can't help but feel joy when you are around her. That's how I felt that whole day as we were surrounded by so much love. In the midst of one of the saddest periods of my life, I was reminded that God always provides a light.

On Wednesday, October 3, I announced the news about my sitcom and my divorce on my radio show. I was not going to give the media the control or benefit of telling my story. I was going to tell it my way. I chose to keep the details of my divorce private. I said only, "The television and news reports about the cause of the split are not true." I admitted that I wished I had never married him and that he had done something terrible to me and I wouldn't stand for it. But I refused to go any further into the details. To defend Esteban would be a lie. To tell the truth would be too horrible.

I missed Esteban as a companion, but I thanked God that I didn't truly love him. If I had, his betrayals would have broken me. I was sad and hurt, but because he never truly had my heart, I knew that I would be okay.

My family had all thought this time the marriage would be forever. I said, "I have an eight-year track record. Trino was eight years, Juan was eight years. Maybe I knew Esteban wasn't going to last forever, but I thought we would at least get the eight years."

When we were going through the divorce, I took off my diamond wedding ring, but I still wore the black-diamond engagement ring.

"Why are you wearing that?" my family would ask.

"Because I always knew I would be a widow."

"But he's not dead."

"He is to me."

I wanted to auction off my engagement and wedding rings to save my friend Chava's life. He was an ex-employee and so dear to me. He had leukemia and needed $200,000 for a bone-marrow transplant.

I announced the auction on my radio show with so much joy, and then Esteban's attorney called my attorney and stated that I could not auction it. They were still negotiating the details of our divorce, and the rings could end up belonging to Esteban. I cried not to be able to hold the auction for Chava. I couldn't believe Esteban would do such a thing, but it only confirmed to me that he was not the man I thought he was.

On December 3, 2012, I delivered a donation check to the Children's Hospital Los Angeles. I was wearing my most ghetto overalls, held together with a safety pin, as I handed over the check. I was so sad about everything that was going on in my life, and it was the one moment that made me feel as if I still had a purpose.

When I left the hospital, my car somehow made its way to Fernando's apartment in Hollywood. I sat out front with my car still in drive, debating whether I should call him. I had not seen him since I'd married Esteban more than two years earlier. Through all of our drama, Fernando was the one man I could talk through all my shit with, and I knew he would never judge or shame me for my mistakes. More important, he was the one man who never betrayed me. On that day, I needed to remind myself that such a man existed. I needed him.

I put the car in park and called him, praying that he'd pick up.

As soon as I heard him say "Hello" I got a lump in my throat.

"Where are you?" I said.

"I'm home. Why?"

"Good. Come outside."

He came outside and got into my passenger seat. I was crying by then.

"What's the matter?"

"I'm divorcing Esteban."

I'm sure he already knew either from his mother or from seeing it all over the media. But he didn't ask me what had happened or why. Instead he made me laugh. Of course.

We got Subway and ate it on the roof of his building overlooking Hollywood and Highland. I told him everything that was going on, down to each embarrassing detail. Though he knew I should never have married Esteban, he never said it. He just let me talk. And then he leaned in and kissed me—a sweet, tender, honest kiss. Sometimes that's all you need from a man: a good kiss, some Subway, and an ear to listen to all of the shit rattling around in your head.

Two days later I went into the radio station to do the weekly show with Rosie. We had our dad on the show that day as a special guest. We reminisced with him about "the good old days" of growing up poor in Long Beach. The Saturdays at the swap meets, selling buttons at concerts and during the 1984 Olympics. He told us again about how he had made it to America and the man at the gas station in San Diego who gave him $20, which made the rest of his life and our lives possible. Afterward Rosie and I went to the swap meet to visit the world we once knew so well, the world that helped to shape us into the adults we became.

As we walked through those old rows of tables, we talked about the sitcom deal. "How is it that these strangers see something in me that is worthy of love, but not the men closest to me?" I asked Rosie.

"You will find love one day," she said. "A true, enduring love."

"You're forgetting, Sister. I already found that love onstage. My fans give me that love."

As we walked the old path that I used to run between my parents' booths, I remembered the simplicity of my childhood. I remembered the years when we had no money and were barely getting by, but we had each other, and that was all that mattered. It was still all that mattered. I was so looking forward to Christmas that year. I wanted everyone to be together again, despite any arguments or differences that we may have had—I wanted every Rivera to be in the same place at the same time. I needed them all. I would always need them all.

In the middle of my reminiscing I turned to Rosie and asked, "Do you want Chinese food? I bet your baby wants Chinese food." What that meant, we both knew, was that I wanted Chinese food even though I was on a diet.

"Yes, I think the baby does want Chinese," Rosie said, since she knew how to play this game so well.

We ordered Chinese food and ate it in my car in an empty parking lot as we talked for hours about everything that was important and not important in life: love, sex, babies, men, a new Runner Boy, God, music, childhood memories, drunken memories, and the dreams of what was still to come.

On December 9, 2012, after performing at a concert in Monterrey, Mexico, Jenni Rivera passed away in a tragic plane crash along with four beloved members of her team—lawyer Mario Macias, publicist Arturo Rivera, makeup artist Jacob Yebale, and hairstylist Jorge "Gigi" Sanchez—as well as the pilots of the plane, Miguel Perez and Alejandro Torres. Jenni had been writing this autobiography for years, but always refused to let it go to print because she didn't know how it should end. The truth is, the story of Jenni Rivera was never meant to have an ending. As with all true icons, her legend will endure for many lifetimes. They will be forever telling the tale of la diva de la banda, la reina de reinas, *the rebel from Long Beach,* la mariposa de barrio, *the badass mother who could not be broken.*

MARIPOSA DE BARRIO

Aquí estoy vengo desde muy lejos,
el camino fue negro pero al fin ya triunfé,
Me arrastré, viví todos los cambios,
y aunque venía llorando mis alas levanté.

Mariposa de barrio, la que vive cantando
La oruga ha transformado, su dolor en color.
Mariposa de barrio que vuela del aplauso
Porque fue donde encontró el verdadero amor
Vive en los escenarios.

Tócame, soy como cualquier otra,
me conquista una rosa aun creo en el amor
Ahora estoy, entre luces hermosas,
mas cuando estaba sola, sé que Dios me cuidó

Mariposa de barrio que vuela del aplauso
Porque fue donde encontró el verdadero amor
Vive en los escenarios.

Porque fue donde encontró el verdadero amor,
mariposa de barrio.

MARIPOSA DE BARRIO

Butterfly of the hood, singing live
the caterpillar has transformed her sadness into color.
Butterfly of the hood, flying from the applause
because it is where she found true love
live, onstage.

Touch me, I am like any other
a conqueror, a rose who believes in love.
Now I am among the beautiful lights
but when I was alone, it was God who took care of me.

Butterfly of the hood, singing live
the caterpillar has transformed her sadness into color.
Butterfly of the hood, flying from the applause
because it is where she found true love
live, onstage.

Because it is where I found true love,
butterfly of the hood.

Todo lo puedo en Cristo que me fortalece.
—Filipenses 4:13

I can do all things through Christ, who gives me strength.
—Philippians 4:13

Acknowledgments

Mariposa de Barrio:

"Thank you, God . . . and thank you, my fans. Gracias a ti, mi público, mi gente, gracias por tu cariño, por tu apoyo, por tu amor, por tú también ser parte de esta, mi vida loca."—Jenni Rivera